INDIAN

CRAFTS

AND LORE

THE COMPLETE BOOK OF
INDIAN CRAFTS AND LORE

BY W. BEN HUNT

gb GOLDEN PRESS · NEW YORK
Western Publishing Company, Inc.
Racine, Wisconsin

HOW TO SAY INDIAN NAMES

Following is a list of Indian names used in this book. Each name is spelled twice—first the way you usually see it, then as it is usually pronounced. The spellings given for pronunciation look a little queer, but if you will pronounce the syllables in the usual way, you will be saying the Indian word correctly. Pronounce the capitalized syllables a little louder than the others; that is, accent them.

Abittibi	ab-i-TIB-ee	**Jemez**	HAY-mess	**Pequot**	PEE-kwat
Abnaki	ab-NAK-ee	**Jicarilla**	hee-ka-REE-ya	**Pima**	PEE-ma
Algonquin	al-GONG-kwin	**Karok**	KAR-ok	**Potawatomi**	pot-a-WAT-o-mee
Alibamu	al-ee-BAM-oo	**Keres**	KAY-res	**Pueblo**	PWEB-lo
Apache	a-PACH-ee	**Kickapoo**	KIK-a-poo	**Quahatika**	kwa-HAT-ti-ka
Arapaho	a-RAP-a-ho	**Kiowa**	KY-o-way	**Quawpaw**	KWAW-paw
Arikara	a-REE-ka-ra	**Klikitat**	KLIK-e-tat	**Sauk**	SAWK
Assiniboin	a-SIN-na-boin	**Kwakiutl**	KWAK-ee-ootl	**Saulteaux**	SAWL-toe
Attacapan	a-TAK-a-pan	**Lipan**	LEE-pan	**Seminole**	SEM-in-ole
Bellacoola	bel-la-KOO-la	**Mandan**	MAN-dan	**Seneca**	SEN-a-ka
Biloxi	be-LOK-see	**Maricopa**	mar-ee-KO-pa	**Shawnee**	SHAW-nee
Blackfoot	(Not Blackfeet)	**Menominee**	me-NOM-in-ee	**Shoshone**	sho-SHO-nee
Cayuga	ka-YOO-ga	**Mescalero**	mes-ka-LAIR-o	**Sioux**	SOO
Chemehuevi	shem-ay-WAY-vee	**Miami**	mi-AM-ee	**Sisseton**	sis-SEE-ton
Cherokee	CHAIR-o-kee	**Micmac**	MIK-mak	**Susquehanna**	sus-kwe-HAN-na
Cheyenne	shy-EN	**Mohave**	Mo-HAH-vay	**Teton**	TEE-ton
Chickasaw	CHICK-a-saw	**Mohawk**	MO-hawk	**Tewa**	TAY-wa
Chipewyan	Chi-POY-an	**Mohican**	mo-HEE-kan	**Tlingit**	TLING-git
Chippewa	CHIP-a-wa	**Muskogee**	mus-KO-gee	**Tonkawa**	TONG-ka-wa
Choctaw	CHOK-taw	**Natchez**	NAT-chess	**Tsimshian**	SIM-she-an
Coast Salish	SAY-lish	**Navaho**	NAH-va-ho	**Tuscarora**	tus-ca-RO-ra
Comanche	ko-MAN-chee	**Nez Perce'**	NAY pair-SAY	**Umatilla**	yoo-ma-TIL-a
Dakota	da-KO-ta	**Nootka**	NOOT-ka	**Walapai**	WAH-la-pie
Delaware	DEL-a-ware	**Oglala**	o-GLA-la	**Walla Walla**	WAH-la WAH-la
Gros Ventre	Grow VAWN-tra	**Ojibwa**	o-JIB-way	**Wenatchi**	we-NACH-ee
Haida	HY-da	**Omaha**	O-ma-ha	**Winnebago**	win-nee-BAY-go
Havasupai	ha-va-SOO-pie	**Oneida**	o-NY-da	**Wyandot**	WY-an-dot
Hidatsa	hee-DAT-sa	**Onondaga**	on-on-DA-ga	**Yakima**	YAK-e-ma
Hopi	HO-pee	**Osage**	O-sayj	**Yankton**	YANG-ton
Hunkpapa	HUNG-pa-pa	**Ottawa**	OT-ta-wa	**Yanktonai**	YANG-ton-eye
Hupa	HOO-pa	**Paiute**	PIE-ute	**Yuchi**	YOO-chee
Huron	HEW-ron	**Papago**	PA-pa-go	**Yuma**	YOO-ma
Iroquois	EAR-o-kwoi	**Pawnee**	paw-NEE	**Zuni**	ZOO-nee

CONTENTS

ABOUT BEN HUNT

The rabbit hunt

There were three things that inspired Ben Hunt to become an expert on handicraft and an Indian lore authority. First was his grandmother, who told him tales of the Indians of the Wisconsin woodlands. She also inspired and encouraged him to draw, to learn whittling, to do leather work, and to make the things he wanted or needed instead of buying them.

The second was Uncle Dan Beard, one of the principal leaders of the Boy Scouts of America, who for years wrote articles on wood lore and handicraft for *Boys' Life* magazine. From these articles Ben got many of the ideas for his boyhood projects.

The third was a band of Sioux Indians which appeared in Milwaukee with the Buffalo Bill Wild West Show. In those days circuses pitched their tents in the old National Park grounds, not far from Ben's home on the south side of Milwaukee. The Indians who set up their tepees behind the circus tents were the first real Indians with whom Ben ever came in contact. They wore buckskin leggings and war bonnets of eagle feathers, and they painted their faces. Many of them were famous warriors who had helped defeat Custer at the Little Big Horn.

Ben was fascinated by them. He hung around their tepees all day, trying to talk to them; but they ignored him completely and continued talking to each other in their native tongue.

"If there was only some way I could figure out how to get these fellows interested in me; if I could only think of something they wanted, I think I could get them to talk," thought Ben.

Suddenly he remembered that there were a lot of rabbits back in the park. He suggested to the Indians that they might like a little wild meat for a change. This was just the right idea! It wasn't very long before a twelve-year-old Milwaukee boy was stalking cottontail rabbits with a band of the wildest Indians that ever came off the Western Plains.

The Indians took him back to their encampment and he was allowed to go into their tepees

Ben Hunt

4

Ben Hunt's cabin

with them. The rabbits were skinned and thrown in the cooking pot for their dinner.

Then the big thrill came. The circus band started to play and it was time for the Big Show. The old chief put his arm around Ben's shoulders and said, "Come." He led Ben right through the performers' entrance into the Big Top, where he was their guest for the Big Show.

"I was the envy of all of the kids in Milwaukee that day, when they saw how friendly those Indians were to me. Never again did I pay to get into a Buffalo Bill Wild West Show."

Among these Indians was Standing Bear of the Wanblee Sioux, who passed away shortly after this book was first published.

This was the beginning of a life-long study of the American Indians, their lore, and their arts and crafts. Ben Hunt has become internationally known as an authority on these subjects.

After he moved to the little town of Hales Corners, where he now lives, he became vitally interested in Boy Scouting. Because of his skill in making things and his ability to explain things on a boy's level, he soon became handicraft instructor of the Hales Corners Boy Scout Troop. Later he became handicraft commissioner for the Milwaukee Area Boy Scout Council.

Each month in *Boys' Life* magazine, the official publication of the Boy Scouts of America, there appear two or three illustrated articles by Ben Hunt on Indian lore and handicraft. His Indian Lore column appears under the name of "Lone Eagle" (Wanblee Isnala); the Whittling and Carving column, under the name of "Whittling Jim"; and the articles on silversmithing

and other handicraft skills under his real name.

Boy Scouts and youth groups all over the world know of Ben Hunt. His workshop is a log cabin built in 1924 in the wood lot behind his Hales Corners home. Originally it was one large room with a fireplace at one end and a homemade stove at the other. It soon was filled with Indian lore and handicraft material. Many of the things were given to Ben by the Indian craftsmen themselves. The cabin is bigger now, and has a kitchen and a combination workshop, library, and office. In the workshop there are always several projects in various stages of completion. As soon as one is completed to Ben's satisfaction, he makes a pen-and-ink drawing of it.

Every other year Ben and his wife take long trips across the country, visiting museums, trading posts, reservations and Indian friends. As a member of *Boys' Life* staff, he attended four National Boy Scout Jamborees, namely, Valley Forge in 1950, Irving Ranch, Calif., in 1953, 2nd Valley Forge in 1957, and Colorado Springs in 1960. At each he had a booth to display examples of his handicraft.

Ben Hunt prides himself on the fact that his work in Indian lore with the boys and girls of America has helped to preserve the Indian arts and crafts—our only truly native culture—so that more people may appreciate this culture.

In making handicraft projects, he always has kept in mind that they must be made from materials readily obtained, and his plans and drawings are made in such a way that boys and girls can easily understand them.

THE EDITORS

ABOUT INDIAN LORE

INDIAN lore has always been popular with boys and girls. Recently there has been a marked increase in the number of youth organizations who have added it to their programs. Some of these units, however, have failed to realize that there is more to an Indian lore program than making costumes. This is only the beginning. If a unit will follow through with a program of dancing, pageantry, and general entertaining, they will have a project that will keep their organization healthy and growing, for it is after the costumes have been made that the fun really begins. The experience of making a few public appearances will set the group to work making new and better costumes, studying more about the Indians, and learning more dances. There is no end to the work and to the fun that can be had. Indian lore, too, is a program that can be shared by many or a few. A single boy or girl in an isolated district can enjoy studying and making Indian costumes. And so can a group of twenty or thirty boys and girls.

Indian lore groups studying the origin of the American Indians soon discover that their past is a part of the history of our own country. Through this hobby a greater understanding and appreciation of the founding and growth of America can be developed.

The making of Indian costumes and the pageantry of Indian dancing has another value, for it is through them that the true primitive arts and culture of our land can be preserved.

Indian lore groups now going through old records and visiting museums gradually have revived some of these arts and crafts to the point where they are appreciated by the real Indians. Some of the books printed on Indian lore subjects are used by the Indians themselves.

Boys working on Indian Lore projects

Boys at Indian Lore pow-wow

It should be pointed out here that the purpose of Indian lore is not to be like Indians, but to enjoy some of their dancing and crafts. It also should be pointed out that Indian lore groups do not pretend to copy authentic Indian crafts and dances. They modify the best of these primitive arts to fit into a boy and girl program.

Indian lore groups have done a lot to teach the general public that Indian lore is a program with a purpose. It is not merely sticking a feather in your hair, jumping up and down, and calling it Indian dancing. Not many people have the opportunity to see a real Indian ceremonial, but in practically every community there is an Indian lore group. The people in these communities who attend an Indian lore program are amazed at the spirit of the group, the beauty of Indian costuming, and the cleverness of the dancing.

There are several things that a group contemplating Indian lore must consider if it is to have a successful program. First, is the amount of time the leader and members will have for the program. It will take a minimum of one night a week for study and handicraft work. Much of the knowledge must come from research in books and magazines, trips to museums, and Indian ceremonials. Many ideas can be gained by contacting other Indian lore groups.

The next question is what kind of an Indian program you want. Your group should decide on what tribe or tribes of Indians you wish to study, and a plan should be prepared. As a general rule the western plains tribes are the most picturesque and the most popular with Indian lore groups. Their feathered war bonnets, beaded war shirts, leggings, moccasins, and dancing have always inspired and attracted boys and girls. I suppose this is because the last great battles between the white men and the Indians took place not so long ago on our western plains. And practically all of the Indians we see in circuses and ceremonies dress in war bonnets and ride ponies in a western plains fashion.

If your group is a large one it should split into different tribes. Each tribe can make the costumes and do the dances of that tribe.

As soon as tribal groups have been set up, work can be started on the costumes. It should be noted here that some sort of decision should be made concerning the number of braves, medicine men, and chiefs that each tribe can have. It looks very silly and ineffective to see an Indian lore group made up of all chiefs and no Indians. Coup feathers should be awarded on the point basis rather than the dollar system.

All of the handicrafts shown in this book were especially designed from authentic Indian articles in such a way that boys and girls would have no trouble making them. If you follow the directions and take your time you will find that you will have little or no difficulty.

7

WHO ARE THE INDIANS?

THERE are many stories and beliefs about the American Indian that are not true. Even the name "Indian" is confusing.

When Columbus landed on the shores of San Salvador, he thought that he had reached the East Indies. In a letter which he wrote in February, 1493, he calls the natives of the island "Indios."

The word "Indios" or "Indian," in spite of its misleading meaning, has passed into common usage in the language of the civilized world. In our English language, we have over two hundred words which use "Indian" as a prefix, such as Indian summer, Indian corn, Indian file, and so forth.

The expression "Red Man" was used to describe the Indian by the white traders. It came from the fact that some of the Indian tribes painted themselves with red oxide. Actually, the color of Indian skin varies from very light yellow or olive color, to very dark brown. Their eyes vary in color from black, brown, or hazel to gray or even blue; their hair from straight, coarse black to soft brown. Some Indians are tall and straight with high cheek bones, while others are short, round, and squat.

Some of the most perplexing questions which have been asked about the American Indian as a people are: Who are the Indians? Where did they come from? How long have they been here?

People who study these things now generally agree that the early ancestors of the Indians came from Asia. There is a strong resemblance between the American Indian and the people of eastern Asia. Even today Asia is separated from North America by only fifty miles of water. Ages ago there may have been a land or ice connection across which some tribes migrated.

During the ice ages, there were evidently periods of time when the glaciers receded. Certain areas were probably free of ice even during the height of the glaciation. These provided routes into North America for wanderers.

Columbus landing on the shores of San Salvador

Undoubtedly there were several migrations from Asia. Some, perhaps, were by such accidents as boats being washed out to sea by storms. Perhaps bands of hunters wandered across the frozen sea in search of game, crossed into Alaska, and then turned southward.

Archaeologists at present believe that man has lived on the North American continent for at least ten thousand years, and possibly for twenty to twenty-five thousand years. It is, of course, impossible to set the exact time.

Ancestors of the American Indians migrating into North America

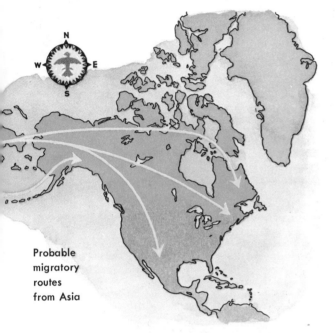

Probable migratory routes from Asia

The best method of establishing that man existed at a certain date is by digging up weapons or skeletons near the remains of extinct animals. (Scientists are now able to compute the approximate ages of these ancient objects by measuring the radioactivity of some of the carbon isotopes in them.)

In 1926, eight miles west of Folsom, New Mexico, a group of paleontologists found two pieces of chipped flint with the fossilized bones of a kind of bison which had been extinct for thousands of years. These pieces of flint have become known as the Folsom Points. Several years later, other similar flint points were found with the skeletons of over twenty large bison. All the bison lacked tail bones, indicating that the animals had been slain by man; for when an animal is skinned its tail is removed.

These Folsom Points are considerably different from more modern flint points. They are pressure flaked, about two inches in length, quite thin, and of good quality workmanship. They are easily distinguished from other arrowheads by the fluted point with grooved channels produced by the removal of a longitudinal flake, giving them a hollow-ground appearance. Since the original discovery, Folsom-type points have been found in many other locations, as far east as the state of Massachusetts, north in Canada, and as far south as Texas. They are among the oldest evidences of man's existence on the North American continent.

Folsom Point

Later Flint Point

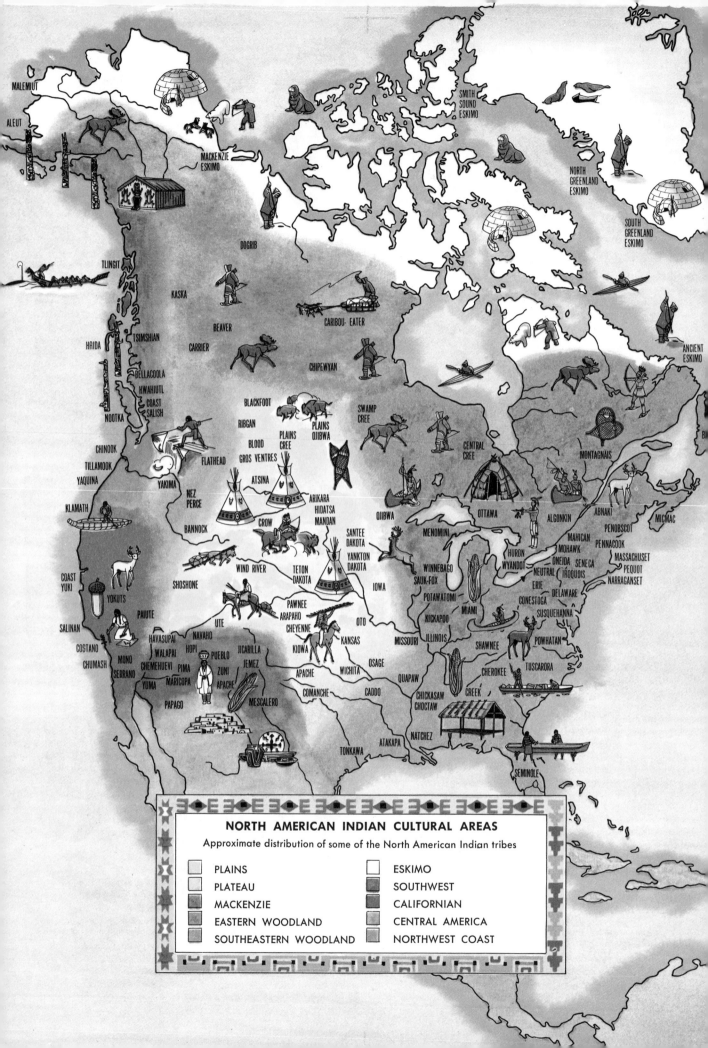

NORTH AMERICAN INDIAN CULTURAL AREAS

Approximate distribution of some of the North American Indian tribes

PLAINS

PLATEAU

MACKENZIE

EASTERN WOODLAND

SOUTHEASTERN WOODLAND

ESKIMO

SOUTHWEST

CALIFORNIAN

CENTRAL AMERICA

NORTHWEST COAST

MALEMIUT

ALEUT

MACKENZIE ESKIMO

SMITH SOUND ESKIMO

NORTH GREENLAND ESKIMO

SOUTH GREENLAND ESKIMO

ANCIENT ESKIMO

TLINGIT

DOGRIB

KASKA

BEAVER

CARIBOU-EATER

HAIDA

TSIMSHIAN

CARRIER

CHIPEWYAN

BELLACOOLA

KWAHIUTL

COAST SALISH

NOOTKA

CHINOOK

BLACKFOOT

RIBGAN

PLAINS CREE

PLAINS OJIBWA

SWAMP CREE

CENTRAL CREE

MONTAGNAIS

BLOOD

GROS VENTRES

TILLAMOOK

YAQUINA

FLATHEAD

ATSINA

ARIKARA

HIDATSA

MANDAN

OJIBWA

OTTAWA

ALGONKIN

ABNAKI

MICMAC

YAKIMA

NEZ PERCE

CROW

SANTEE DAKOTA

YANKTON DAKOTA

MENOMINI

HURON

WYANDOT

MAHICAN

MOHAWK

ONEIDA

NEUTRAL

IROQUOIS

SENECA

PENOBSCOT

PENNACOOK

MASSACHUSET

PEQUOT

NARRAGANSET

KLAMATH

BANNOCK

WIND RIVER

TETON DAKOTA

IOWA

WINNEBAGO

SAUK-FOX

ERIE

DELAWARE

CONESTOGA

SUSQUEHANNA

COAST YUKI

YOKUTS

SHOSHONE

PAWNEE

ARAPAHO

CHEYENNE

OTO

POTAWATOMI

MIAMI

POWHATAN

PAIUTE

UTE

NAVAHO

KIOWA

KANSAS

MISSOURI

KICKAPOO

ILLINOIS

SHAWNEE

SALINAN

HAVASUPAI

WALAPAI

HOPI

JICARILLA

TUSCARORA

COSTANO

MONO

SERRANO

CHEMEHUEVI

PIMA

PUEBLO

ZUNI

JEMEZ

APACHE

OSAGE

QUAPAW

CHEROKEE

CHUMASH

YUMA

MARICOPA

APACHE

WICHITA

CREEK

PAPAGO

MESCALERO

COMANCHE

CADDO

CHICKASAW

CHOCTAW

TONKAWA

ATAKAPA

NATCHEZ

SEMINOLE

ABOUT INDIAN TRIBES

EXPERTS have listed all Indian tribes that lived in the same way into groups. These groups are called cultural areas. There are ten of these areas in the North American continent. In the United States proper, we have seven distinctive cultural areas: the Eastern Woodland, the Southeastern, the Plains, the Southwestern, the Plateau, the California, and the North Pacific Coast. (See map.) There are about thirty different language families spoken by these groups, and about six hundred dialects.

The names given Indian tribal divisions usually are corruptions of native names by the Spanish, French, or Americans; nicknames of one tribe for another; or incorrect translations of native names or nicknames. Most of these names are not used by the Indians themselves except when talking to the white man. The Indian name for themselves is usually their tribal word for "Men" or for "People."

It is very difficult to keep track of the true native names of Indian tribes. Mistakes which were made before the native languages were studied have become accepted as facts.

As an example of how mixed-up Indian tribal names can be, consider the name of the Chippewa tribe. In early writings, it was incorrectly stated that the name was derived from the Chippewa word "O-jib-ub-way" meaning "to roast until puckered up," after the tribal style of moccasins with puckered seams. It is now accepted that the word "Ojibwa" (Ojibway) is a corruption of the tribe's word "O-jib-i-weg,"

meaning "those who draw pictures or pictographs." The tribal word for "Chippewa" is "Ah-nee-she-nah-be," meaning "first man."

Another example is the word "Sioux" (pronounced Soo) which is the American corruption of part of a French corruption of the Ojibwa name for that tribe. The Ojibwa call the Sioux "Na-do-wes-si-weg," meaning "snake" or "enemy." The French changed this name to "Na-do-wes-si-oux" (Na-do-wes-see-oo), and early in the 1800's the Americans took the last two syllables, "Si-oux" of the French name, and pronounced it "Soo." To complicate things further, the tribal name for themselves is "Dakota" or "Lakota" depending on what dialect was being used. This word, in native tongue, means "allies."

Another Indian name that has confused many people, and is probably the most misused name applied to Indians, is the name "Siwash" (Sy-wash). There never has been a Siwash tribe, nor is there one now. This name is the corruption of the French word "sauvage" (so-vahj) which means "savage." In the early days of the exploration of the Northwest, there developed a trade language which was called "Chinook." It was a jargon made up of a combination of Indian and non-Indian words. In this made-up language, the word for Indian was Si-wash, to distinguish him from white man.

To help you pronounce the various Indian names, you will find on page 2 a chart listing many of the tribes.

11

THE GOLDEN EAGLE

THE GOLDEN EAGLE is the finest and noblest bird found in North America. He measures from 30 to 40 inches in height and has a wing spread of from 7 to 7½ feet. His war cry can be heard from Alaska to lower California. Because of the Golden Eagle's great strength and courage, the American Indian admired this bird and prized his feathers above all other adornments.

The thirteen tail feathers of the adult bird were considered to possess great medicine. These feathers, which are white with dark brown tips, measure 12 to 14 inches in length. The eagle's wing feathers (pinion feathers) were also used for war bonnets, bustles, and other ceremonial regalia. Many times the Indian would make an entire war bonnet from one eagle, using the long tail feathers in the front, and the wing feathers in graduated sizes down the back. The right wing feathers would be used on the right side of the bonnet, and the left wing feathers on the left side of the bonnet.

The plumes or fluff feathers that grow at the base of the bird's tail were used by the Indians for the base of the larger feathers. The two largest plumes from the bird were called breath feathers by the Indians because of their lightness; the slightest breath would cause them to move as though they were breathing. These two feathers were sometimes 8 inches long and were valued as highly as brown-tipped tail feathers.

Because the Golden eagle and the Bald eagle were facing extinction, the Audubon Society, with the help of naturalists, encouraged Congress to enact laws protecting them. It is now against the law to trap or shoot eagles, or to have in one's possession unprocessed eagle feathers. Therefore, today we must use imitations.

White turkey wing and tail feathers, with the tips dyed brown, may be used. For tips and fluffs, the turkey marabou or fluffs make suitable substitutes for real eagle fluffs.

There were several methods by which the Indians obtained eagle feathers. Some tribes dug a pit in the ground in areas known to have eagles. These pits were large enough to conceal a brave. The trap was baited with a live rabbit or pieces of buffalo meat, and the opening was covered with a buffalo hide or brush. A large enough opening was left so that the Indian crouching in the pit could grab the tail feathers of the bird alighting to take the bait. The bird would lose its feathers, but could escape unharmed to grow new tail feathers by its next moulting period. This method was very dangerous. Often bears, attracted by the bait, would discover and kill the Indian. Sometimes eagles

Brave being attacked by bear

12

Eagle in captivity

were caught and killed for their feathers, plumes, and claws.

There also were tribes who captured young eagles while they were still in the nest. These birds were tethered by a leather thong around their leg and were kept solely for their feathers; they were plucked regularly. These birds seldom became tame and never lost their desire for freedom. They continually would fly into the air as far as the leather thong would allow, screaming their defiance at their captor.

Regardless of where or how an Indian brave accumulated feathers, he was not allowed, according to tribal law, to wear them until he won them by a brave deed. He had to appear before the tribal council and tell or re-enact his exploit. Witnesses were examined and if in the eyes of the council the deed was thought to be worthy, the brave was authorized to wear the feather or feathers in his hair or war bonnet.

These honors were called "counting coup" (pronounced "coo"). Deeds of exceptional valor (such as to touch the enemy without killing him and escape) were called "grand coup" and were rated more than one feather. Sometimes a tuft of horsehair or down was added to the tip of a feather to designate additional honor. Some tribes designated special deeds by special marking on "coup" feathers, such as cutting notches or adding paint spots.

The coup feathers of the American Indian can be compared to the campaign ribbons and medals awarded to our modern soldier. An Indian would rather part with his horse, his tepee, or even his wife, than to lose his eagle feathers. To do so would be to be dishonored in the eyes of the tribe. Many old Indian chiefs, such as Many Coup of the Crow tribe, had won enough honors to wear a double-tailed bonnet that dragged on the ground and to carry a feathered lance to display the additional feathers.

Counting coup at tribal council

13

PREPARING FEATHERS

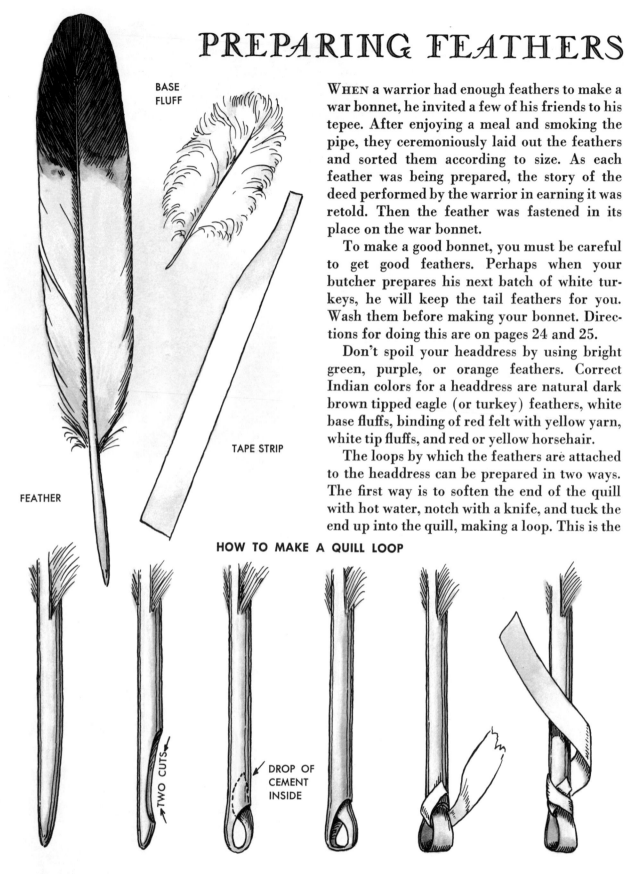

BASE
FLUFF

TAPE STRIP

FEATHER

WHEN a warrior had enough feathers to make a war bonnet, he invited a few of his friends to his tepee. After enjoying a meal and smoking the pipe, they ceremoniously laid out the feathers and sorted them according to size. As each feather was being prepared, the story of the deed performed by the warrior in earning it was retold. Then the feather was fastened in its place on the war bonnet.

To make a good bonnet, you must be careful to get good feathers. Perhaps when your butcher prepares his next batch of white turkeys, he will keep the tail feathers for you. Wash them before making your bonnet. Directions for doing this are on pages 24 and 25.

Don't spoil your headdress by using bright green, purple, or orange feathers. Correct Indian colors for a headdress are natural dark brown tipped eagle (or turkey) feathers, white base fluffs, binding of red felt with yellow yarn, white tip fluffs, and red or yellow horsehair.

The loops by which the feathers are attached to the headdress can be prepared in two ways. The first way is to soften the end of the quill with hot water, notch with a knife, and tuck the end up into the quill, making a loop. This is the

HOW TO MAKE A QUILL LOOP

TWO CUTS

DROP OF
CEMENT
INSIDE

1. SOFTEN END OF QUILL IN HOT WATER AND CUT AS SHOWN WITH SHARP KNIFE.

2. PUT A DROP OF CEMENT ON END AND TUCK IT UP INTO THE QUILL.

3. LET IT DRY. ANCHOR TAPE AND WRAP AS SHOWN ABOVE.

14

method generally used by the Indians. (See pictures below.)

A second method, which is easier for boys and makes a more substantial loop, is to cement a ¼-inch strip of thin leather or rawhide to the quill and then wrap it with adhesive tape. (See page 18.)

The next step is to attach the base fluffs. One way to do this is shown here. You will see another way to do it on page 18.

It is a good idea to put more than one fluff in the front of each quill, because a properly made bonnet should have a heavy bank of fluffs running along the base of all the quill feathers.

After all of the feathers have been prepared in this fashion they should be attached to a skull cap made from the crown of an old felt hat. Be sure not to cut it too skimpy, or it will slide off the head. It should come well down over the ears and should be fitted several times to be sure it is right. On page 17 are directions for lacing the quills to the cap.

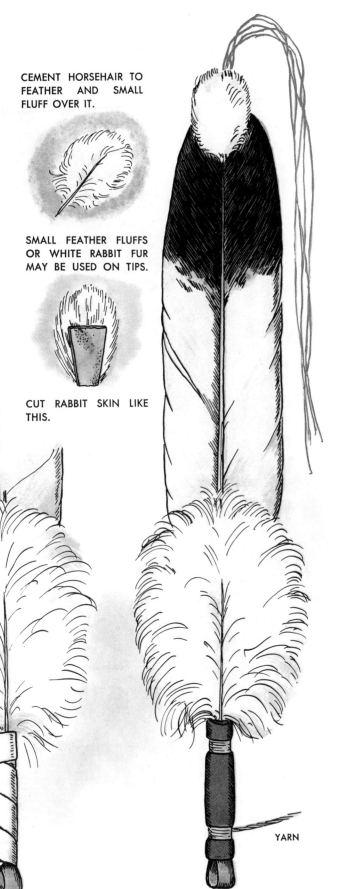

CEMENT HORSEHAIR TO FEATHER AND SMALL FLUFF OVER IT.

SMALL FEATHER FLUFFS OR WHITE RABBIT FUR MAY BE USED ON TIPS.

CUT RABBIT SKIN LIKE THIS.

YARN

4. AT THIS POINT THE BASE FLUFF SHOULD BE ADDED. CEMENT IT TO THE QUILL.

5. CONTINUE WRAPPING WITH YOUR TAPE AS SHOWN.

6. THEN WRAP WITH RED FELT OR FLANNEL. CEMENT EDGE AND WRAP WITH YELLOW YARN.

15

⅛″ BRASS
TUBING

A

TWO OF
THESE
PENDANTS
MAY BE
HUNG JUST
AHEAD OF
THE
ROSETTES.

THE WAR BONNET

THE most colorful item of headwear of any people in the world is the large feathered war bonnet of the American Indian. In the early days it was worn only by the Plains tribes. It was very practical on the plains because there were no bushes or trees for it to catch on. Nowadays when we see the war bonnet used by the Woodland and the Southwestern Indians, we know it has been adopted by these tribes in modern times. Because it is the most picturesque piece of Indian headwear, most people viewing Indian ceremonies expect to see it.

The war bonnet of the Sioux tribe had a large flare to it, while the Crow tribe's bonnet sloped back flatter on the head. The Blackfoot made a bonnet in which the feathers stood straight up from the head.

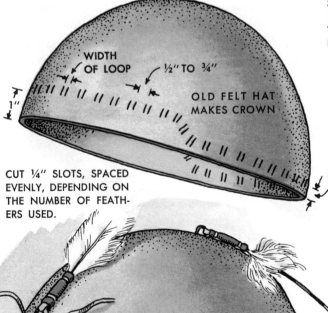

WIDTH OF LOOP   ½" TO ¾"

1"

OLD FELT HAT MAKES CROWN

CUT ¼" SLOTS, SPACED EVENLY, DEPENDING ON THE NUMBER OF FEATHERS USED.

½"

DOTTED LINE SHOWS POSITION OF BEADED BROWBAND AND ROSETTES AND ALSO THE MAJOR PLUME. FOR BEADWORK, SEE PP. 58-65.

AFTER FEATHERS ARE LACED TO HAT, THEY SHOULD BE STRUNG AS SHOWN ON NEXT PAGE "A." USE A DARNING NEEDLE AND WAXED CORD. START AT FRONT AND WORK BOTH WAYS TO THE BACK. ADJUST PROPERLY AND KNOT ENDS.

START LACING QUILLS AT CENTER FRONT. THERE ARE LEFT AND RIGHT FEATHERS. SELECT ACCORDINGLY.

MAJOR PLUME IS A STRIPPED QUILL. IT MAY BE PAINTED OR WRAPPED WITH SEVERAL COLORS OF THREAD OR YARN. FLUFFS ARE TIED ON.

A BONNET CAN HAVE FROM 30 TO 40 FEATHERS DEPENDING ON SIZE OF CROWN, WIDTH OF THE FEATHERS, AND PERSONAL TASTE.

DOUBLE-TAILED WAR BONNET

Some of the famous warriors of the Western Plains earned more coup feathers in their lifetime than were required for a full-sized headdress. These warriors were allowed by tribal law to make and wear a war bonnet having either a single or double row of eagle feathers hanging down the back.

Originally these bonnets were only knee length, but when the Indian started to ride horses, the tails were extended to the wearer's heels.

Use as many feathers as you need for your height. A bonnet having twenty-five feathers on each side of the strip is just right for a boy 6 feet tall. Start at the top with the largest feather and graduate them in size as you work toward the bottom. The bottom of the felt strip should be about 1 inch from the ground.

Remember that only the great and important men of the tribes had the right to wear the double-tailed war bonnet. In any Indian lore group, there should be only one or two warriors allowed to wear this type of headdress.

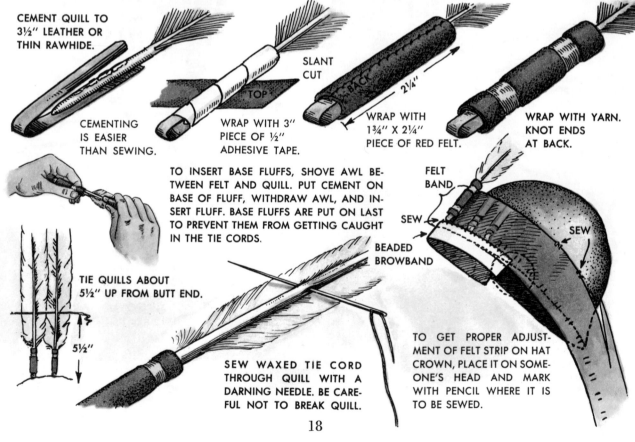

CEMENT QUILL TO 3½" LEATHER OR THIN RAWHIDE.

CEMENTING IS EASIER THAN SEWING.

WRAP WITH 3" PIECE OF ½" ADHESIVE TAPE.

SLANT CUT

TOP

BACK 2¼"

WRAP WITH 1¾" X 2¼" PIECE OF RED FELT.

WRAP WITH YARN. KNOT ENDS AT BACK.

TO INSERT BASE FLUFFS, SHOVE AWL BETWEEN FELT AND QUILL. PUT CEMENT ON BASE OF FLUFF, WITHDRAW AWL, AND INSERT FLUFF. BASE FLUFFS ARE PUT ON LAST TO PREVENT THEM FROM GETTING CAUGHT IN THE TIE CORDS.

TIE QUILLS ABOUT 5½" UP FROM BUTT END.

5½"

SEW WAXED TIE CORD THROUGH QUILL WITH A DARNING NEEDLE. BE CAREFUL NOT TO BREAK QUILL.

FELT BAND

SEW

SEW

BEADED BROWBAND

TO GET PROPER ADJUSTMENT OF FELT STRIP ON HAT CROWN, PLACE IT ON SOMEONE'S HEAD AND MARK WITH PENCIL WHERE IT IS TO BE SEWED.

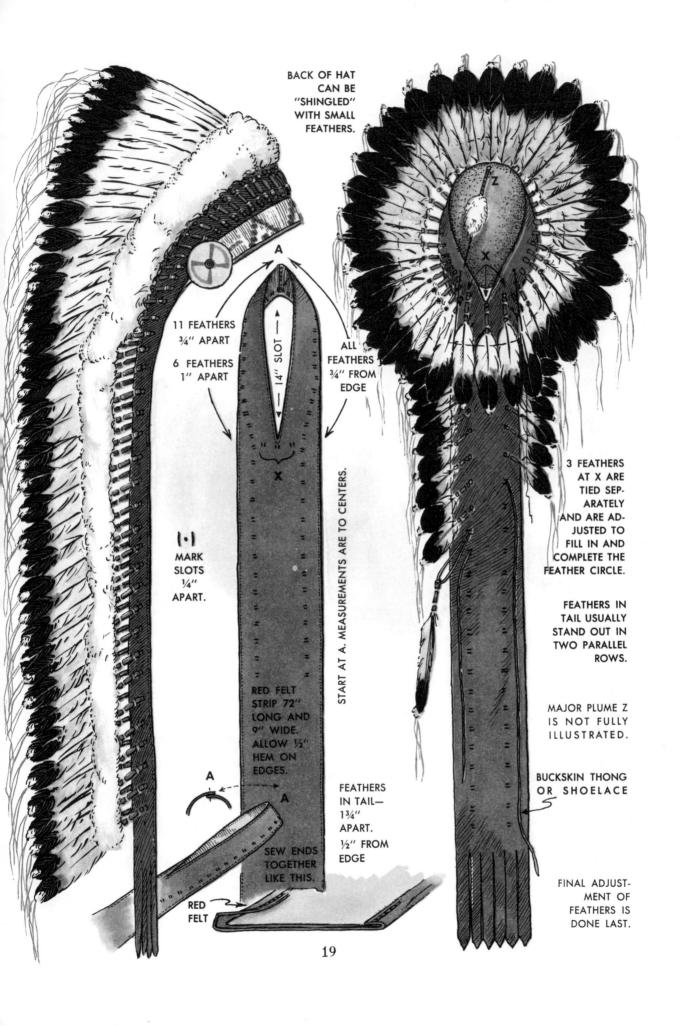

BACK OF HAT
CAN BE
"SHINGLED"
WITH SMALL
FEATHERS.

11 FEATHERS
¾" APART

6 FEATHERS
1" APART

ALL
FEATHERS
¾" FROM
EDGE

A

←14" SLOT→

X

(•)
MARK
SLOTS
¼"
APART.

START AT A. MEASUREMENTS ARE TO CENTERS.

RED FELT
STRIP 72"
LONG AND
9" WIDE.
ALLOW ½"
HEM ON
EDGES.

A
A

SEW ENDS
TOGETHER
LIKE THIS.

RED
FELT

FEATHERS
IN TAIL—
1¾"
APART.
½" FROM
EDGE

Z

X

3 FEATHERS
AT X ARE
TIED SEP-
ARATELY
AND ARE AD-
JUSTED TO
FILL IN AND
COMPLETE THE
FEATHER CIRCLE.

FEATHERS IN
TAIL USUALLY
STAND OUT IN
TWO PARALLEL
ROWS.

MAJOR PLUME Z
IS NOT FULLY
ILLUSTRATED.

BUCKSKIN THONG
OR SHOELACE

FINAL ADJUST-
MENT OF
FEATHERS IS
DONE LAST.

19

THE HORNED WAR BONNET

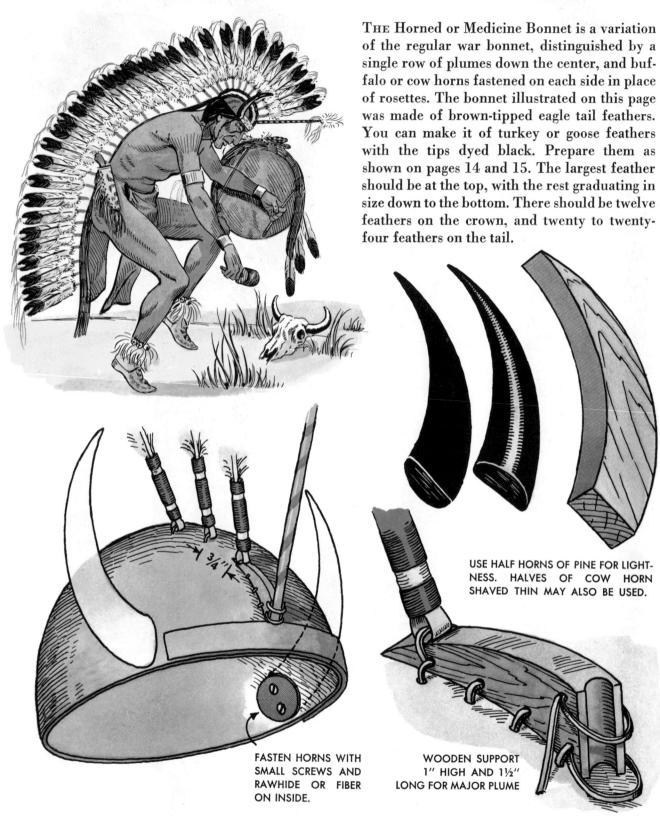

THE Horned or Medicine Bonnet is a variation of the regular war bonnet, distinguished by a single row of plumes down the center, and buffalo or cow horns fastened on each side in place of rosettes. The bonnet illustrated on this page was made of brown-tipped eagle tail feathers. You can make it of turkey or goose feathers with the tips dyed black. Prepare them as shown on pages 14 and 15. The largest feather should be at the top, with the rest graduating in size down to the bottom. There should be twelve feathers on the crown, and twenty to twenty-four feathers on the tail.

USE HALF HORNS OF PINE FOR LIGHTNESS. HALVES OF COW HORN SHAVED THIN MAY ALSO BE USED.

FASTEN HORNS WITH SMALL SCREWS AND RAWHIDE OR FIBER ON INSIDE.

WOODEN SUPPORT 1" HIGH AND 1½" LONG FOR MAJOR PLUME

PREPARE FEATHERS AS SHOWN IN DOUBLE-TAILED BONNET, ATTACHING BASE FLUFFS ON BOTH SIDES OF QUILLS AFTER ADJUSTING CORD IS ATTACHED.

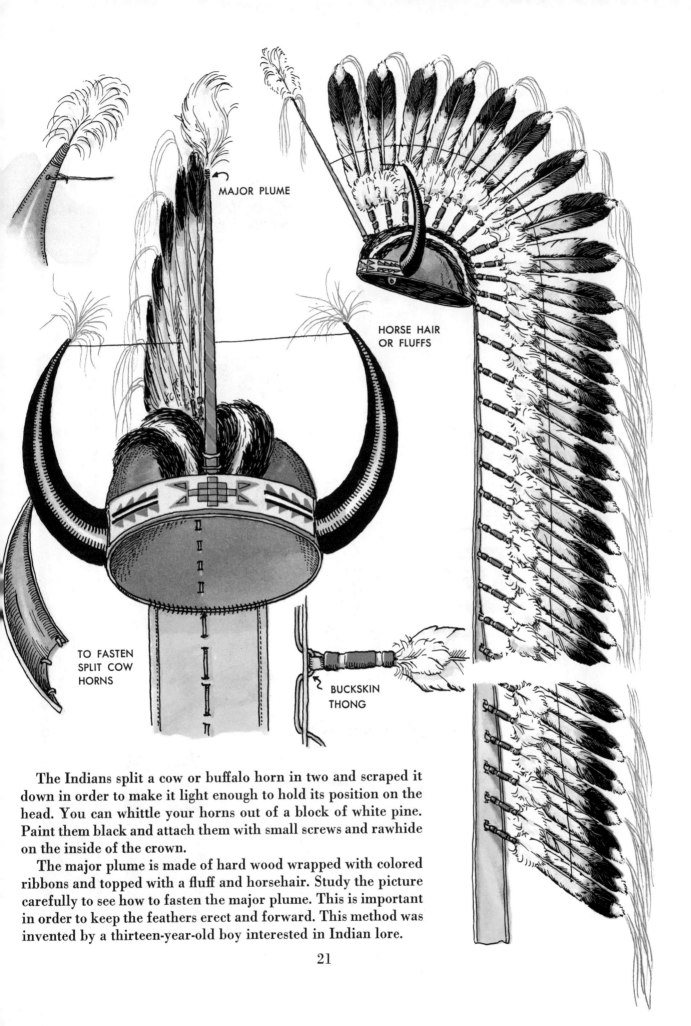

MAJOR PLUME

HORSE HAIR
OR FLUFFS

TO FASTEN
SPLIT COW
HORNS

BUCKSKIN
THONG

The Indians split a cow or buffalo horn in two and scraped it down in order to make it light enough to hold its position on the head. You can whittle your horns out of a block of white pine. Paint them black and attach them with small screws and rawhide on the inside of the crown.

The major plume is made of hard wood wrapped with colored ribbons and topped with a fluff and horsehair. Study the picture carefully to see how to fasten the major plume. This is important in order to keep the feathers erect and forward. This method was invented by a thirteen-year-old boy interested in Indian lore.

21

WAR BONNET STORAGE CASE

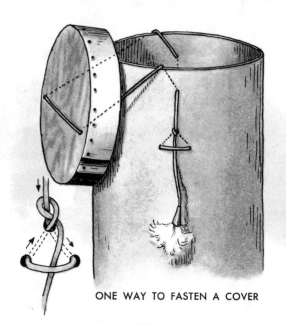

ONE WAY TO FASTEN A COVER

ROLL UP DOUBLE-TAILED BONNETS LIKE THIS.

MOTH BALLS

ANY OF THESE DESIGNS CAN BE REPEATED 3 OR 4 TIMES ON A CASE.

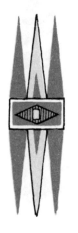    

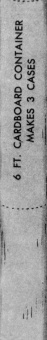

6 FT. CARDBOARD CONTAINER MAKES 3 CASES

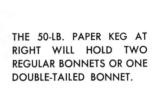

THE 50-LB. PAPER KEG AT RIGHT WILL HOLD TWO REGULAR BONNETS OR ONE DOUBLE-TAILED BONNET.

7" FURNACE PIPE (ALUMINUM OR GALVANIZED)

CUT OFF FOR COVER

9" CARDBOARD CONTAINER WITH COVER

THIS IS HOW BOTTOMS AND COVERS ARE USUALLY MADE AT THE FACTORY.

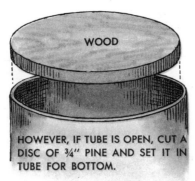

HOWEVER, IF TUBE IS OPEN, CUT A DISC OF ¾" PINE AND SET IT IN TUBE FOR BOTTOM.

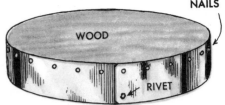

NAILS

WOOD

RIVET

MAKE A SNUG FITTING COVER OF WOOD AND GALVANIZED IRON, ALUMINUM OR ANY OTHER METAL. RIVET AT THE OVERLAP.

IN spite of all the hours of work that go into making an Indian war bonnet, it probably receives less care than any other part of an Indian costume. Usually it is hung on a nail or thrown into a corner where in no time at all the feathers become broken and dirty. A good bonnet should have a good case, for bonnets kept in cases will last indefinitely.

The best material for making a case is a 6- or 8-inch tube used to ship linoleum, or a round cardboard container from sweeping compounds or powders. These can be obtained at your hardware store.

The case can be painted in any design you select. Use a rawhide color for the base, and paint your own Indian symbols on the outside. The decorations on page 22 were taken from paintings on cases made by Plains Indians.

In the bottom of the case, keep a small perforated tin box or bag of moth balls or crystals. Feathers make good food for insects.

To store the bonnet, roll it up, as shown, so that it will slide easily into the case and be fully protected until the next pow wow. Bonnet cases also make good seats, while waiting for your turn in the Indian ceremonies.

TO WASH FEATHERS AND FLUFFS

1. SOAK IN COLD WATER FOR 2 DAYS. WORK OFF DIRT WITH YOUR FINGERS. DO NOT USE A BRUSH.

2. PAT GENTLY IN LUKEWARM MILD SOAP-SUDS, UNTIL ALL DIRT AND STAINS ARE REMOVED.

D A N G E R ! BECAUSE OF GASOLINE FUMES AND DUST FROM PLASTER OF PARIS OR SAWDUST THE JOB OF CLEANING FEATHERS SHOULD BE DONE OUTDOORS.

3. RINSE TWICE IN CLEAN LUKEWARM WATER.

DO NOT USE SAWDUST FROM SOFT WOOD BECAUSE IT CONTAINS RESIN WHICH IS DISSOLVED BY THE GASOLINE.

4. WASH OUTDOORS IN NAPHTHA OR WHITE GASOLINE. THIS WILL ALSO LESSEN THE DANGER OF MOTHS LATER ON. DRAIN OFF MOST OF THE GASOLINE.

5. COVER WITH DRY PLASTER OF PARIS OR HARDWOOD SAWDUST TO ABSORB REMAINING MOISTURE. THEN BRUSH WELL.

6. WASH FLUFFS THE SAME WAY AS YOU DID FEATHERS. FOR DRYING, USE CYLINDER SHOWN ON NEXT PAGE.

EXPERIMENT WITH SEVERAL FEATHERS BEFORE DOING THE ENTIRE BATCH.

FEATHER CARE

THE authentic Indian bonnets that you see usually have a slightly yellowish cast from the smoke of tepee and council fires. The Indians had no way of cleaning their feathers, other than to give them a very light coat of oil. You, however, may want to clean yours occasionally.

First you must remove all of the feathers from the bonnet and wash them according to the directions on the opposite page. Try out one of the back feathers to see whether the naphtha will loosen the adhesive. If it does, you will have to remove the wrappings around the base of the feathers. Follow all directions carefully.

Be sure to examine each feather carefully and replace any broken ones. Turkey feathers occasionally break where they have been sewn.

After reassembling the feathers, oil them lightly with your fingertips. Any unsalted animal grease is good for this job. It keeps the feathers from drying out and restores their natural oils. Birds oil their feathers from the ducts at the tips of their tails. This is known as preening, and the bird is not picking insects, as most people suppose.

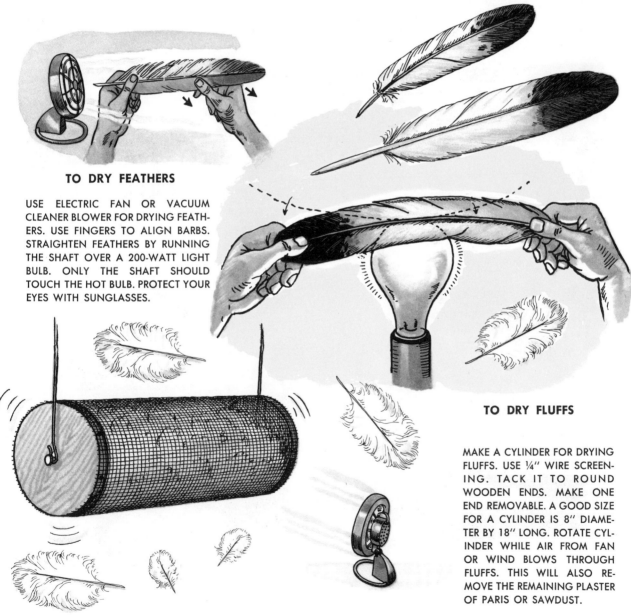

TO DRY FEATHERS

USE ELECTRIC FAN OR VACUUM CLEANER BLOWER FOR DRYING FEATHERS. USE FINGERS TO ALIGN BARBS. STRAIGHTEN FEATHERS BY RUNNING THE SHAFT OVER A 200-WATT LIGHT BULB. ONLY THE SHAFT SHOULD TOUCH THE HOT BULB. PROTECT YOUR EYES WITH SUNGLASSES.

TO DRY FLUFFS

MAKE A CYLINDER FOR DRYING FLUFFS. USE ¼" WIRE SCREENING. TACK IT TO ROUND WOODEN ENDS. MAKE ONE END REMOVABLE. A GOOD SIZE FOR A CYLINDER IS 8" DIAMETER BY 18" LONG. ROTATE CYLINDER WHILE AIR FROM FAN OR WIND BLOWS THROUGH FLUFFS. THIS WILL ALSO REMOVE THE REMAINING PLASTER OF PARIS OR SAWDUST.

ROACH HEADDRESS

ANOTHER type of headdress worn by both Plains and Woodlands Indians was the roach. This was a crest of dyed horsehair fastened to a decorated head harness and topped by a single feather.

Good fibers for you to use in making a roach are tampico, manila, or sisal fibers. Tampico fiber is the best because its fibers are uniform and take dye well. It may be purchased from a brush manufacturer. Whichever fiber you use, you should dye it red on the tips and black along the lower edges.   (See picture.)

When making the fiber bunches, allow about 10 or 12 bunches to one inch. Be careful not to make them too thick. It is much better to have a double row of smaller bunches than a single row of larger ones. The closer and more evenly the bunches are tied together, the smoother your roach will be. A well made roach should ripple back and forth in motion when it is worn.

The roach, like the war bonnet, should be carefully stored away when not in use. The best method I know is to wrap it on a stick, as shown, shaping the fibers downward, and wrapping it completely in a 2-inch strip of protective cloth. By using this method of storage, you will never have to worry about its losing its shape.

If your hair is not black, you may want a cap to wear with your roach. The picture shows how to make one out of a stocking top.

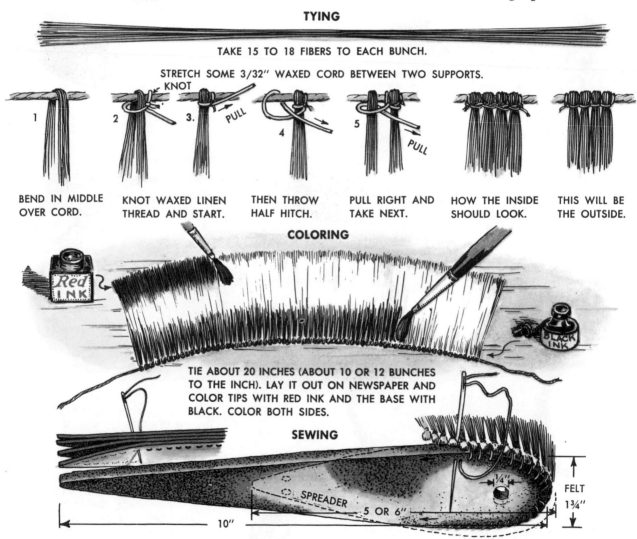

TYING

TAKE 15 TO 18 FIBERS TO EACH BUNCH.

STRETCH SOME 3/32" WAXED CORD BETWEEN TWO SUPPORTS.

KNOT

1 — BEND IN MIDDLE OVER CORD.

2 — KNOT WAXED LINEN THREAD AND START.

3 — PULL — THEN THROW HALF HITCH.

4 — PULL RIGHT AND TAKE NEXT.

5 — PULL — HOW THE INSIDE SHOULD LOOK.

THIS WILL BE THE OUTSIDE.

COLORING

Red INK

BLACK INK

TIE ABOUT 20 INCHES (ABOUT 10 OR 12 BUNCHES TO THE INCH). LAY IT OUT ON NEWSPAPER AND COLOR TIPS WITH RED INK AND THE BASE WITH BLACK. COLOR BOTH SIDES.

SEWING

SPREADER

5 OR 6"

10"

¼"

FELT 1¾"

CUT BASE OF ¼" FELT, OR SEW 4 PIECES OF REGULAR FELT TOGETHER. PUNCH HOLE. THEN CUT A PIECE OF STIFF LEATHER OR FIBER ¼" LARGER AROUND THE FRONT AND SIDES, TAPERING AS SHOWN, FOR THE SPREADER. PUNCH HOLE TO LINE UP WITH HOLE IN BASE.

MOUNTING

TIE BACK OF ROACH HERE

CAP MADE OF TOP OF STOCKING MAY BE SEWED INSIDE HARNESS.

SPREADER

ROACH BASE

HOW ROACH IS PUT TOGETHER

LARGE BEADS

2¼" ¼"

TIN DISCS WITH SHINY SIDES OUT. BACKS PAINTED BRIGHT RED.

FEATHER SOCKET OF CHICKEN LEG BONE, OR BRASS CARTRIDGE SHELL.

PULL FEATHER DOWN AND TIE ENDS TO-GETHER.

FIBER OR RAWHIDE

SPREADER

BASE

1"

LEATHER THONGS

STORING

COVER BROWBAND OF HAR-NESS WITH BEADED BAND OR WIDE STRIP OF FUR. OTHER DECORATIONS, SUCH AS RO-SETTES AND PENDANTS, MAY ALSO BE ADDED TO THE BROW-BAND.

1⅛"

18"

PLACE ON STICK AND WRAP WITH 2" STRIP OF CLOTH

BREECHCLOUTS, APRONS, AND LEGGINGS

UNTIL about sixty or seventy years ago, the breechclout was the primary garment the Indian wore around camp, on hunting trips, or on the warpath.

The breechclout hangs from a belt around the waist. It is about one foot wide and about 6 feet in length, depending on the size of the person wearing it. In the early days the Indians made breechclouts from soft deerskin or buffalo skin, but later on they began to use red and blue blanket material or trade cloth. You can make your breechclout out of outing flannel, broadcloth, suede, blanket material, or velveteen. Dyed tan, these materials make a very

APRONS

APRONS, RATHER THAN BREECHCLOUTS, ARE WORN BY WOODLAND INDIANS.

BREECHCLOUTS

BREECHCLOUTS, WORN BY PLAINS INDIANS, CAN BE MADE OF BUCKSKIN, SUEDE, OR CLOTH.

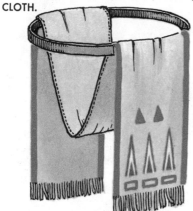

DO NOT ATTEMPT TO FRINGE CLOTH. INSTEAD BIND THE EDGES WITH BIAS TAPE OR RIBBON TO PREVENT PULLING OUT OF SHAPE.

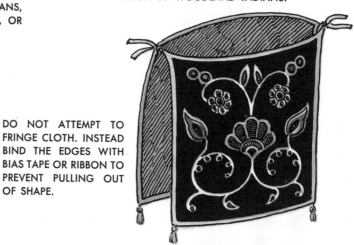

WOODLAND DESIGNS

PLAINS DESIGNS

BREECHCLOUTS ARE NARROWER THAN APRONS AND HANG FROM WAISTBAND.

APRONS ARE SQUARE AND ARE TIED AT THE HIPS. BACK AND FRONT ARE OFTEN DESIGNED DIFFERENTLY.

good substitute for buckskin. The cloth should be plain rather than patterned, for it will be beaded or appliqued with felt Indian designs later.

Often, aprons were used instead of breech-clouts. They are made of dark cloth and decorated with beadwork. The edges should be bound with matching bias tape.

Leggings were also originally made out of soft leather, but later on the Indians made them out of the blanket cloth issued by our Government. For your leggings, you can substitute blue denim or dyed outing flannel.

Today, Indians and those interested in Indian lore are making leggings in the form of trousers. The breechclout goes over the front and back of the belt, as shown on page 28. If you use the old type leggings (see pictures below) and breechclout, you must wear swim trunks underneath. Yes, sir!

LEGGINGS

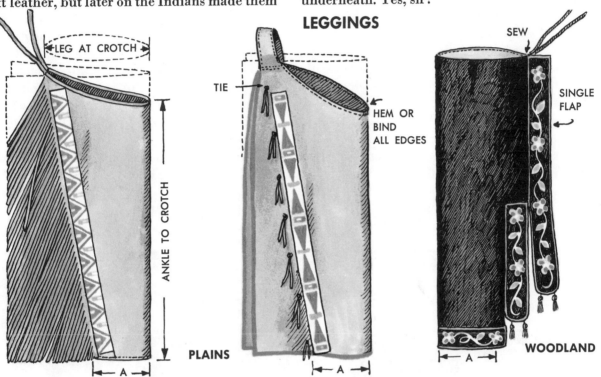

"A" IS JUST WIDE ENOUGH FOR FOOT TO GO THROUGH.

FRINGED LEGGINGS CAN BE MADE OF BUCKSKIN, SUEDE, OR SPLIT COWHIDE. THOSE WITH FLAPS CAN BE MADE OF OUTING FLANNEL DYED TO LOOK LIKE BUCKSKIN OR OF OTHER DARK BLUE OR BLACK CLOTH.

THESE ARE CEREMONIAL LEGGINGS MADE OF BLACK CLOTH. THE BUCKSKIN ONES ARE CUT LIKE THE PLAINS INDIANS BUT WITH SHORT FRINGE AND ONLY A BEADED CUFF.

LEGGING STRIPS

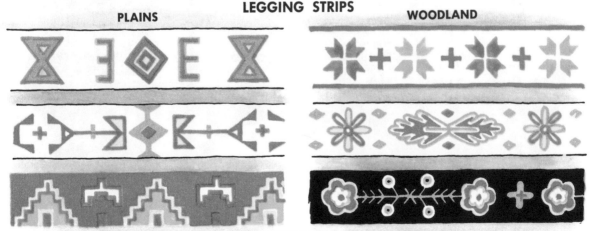

REPEAT THESE DESIGNS FOR ENTIRE STRIP.

WAR SHIRTS

Practically all of the Indian tribes wore some form of shirt. This garment is usually mistakenly called a "war shirt." In reality it was a ceremonial shirt usually worn by the older men or chiefs of authority on solemn occasions.

The Dakotas and Cheyennes trimmed their shirts with small hanks of horsehair. Sometimes human hair was used. These shirts were called "scalp shirts" by the white man, who believed that all the hair decorations were from scalp locks. The Blackfoot and some of the other tribes decorated their shirts with strips of white weasel skin.

Indians on the warpath did not wear shirts. They wore only a breechclout, leggings, and moccasins. War shirts were not worn for active dancing, either, because they were too hot.

Indians made their shirts out of soft buckskin. It usually took two hides for one shirt. Sometimes an additional hide was required for the sleeves. You can make your shirt out of heavy outing flannel or unbleached muslin dyed light brown or ecru. Do not iron it because the rough, unpressed cloth will look more like buckskin. To prevent stretching and raveling, the edges of the shirts should be hemmed or bound with bias tape if they are not fringed.

The Indians used a countless variety of designs and materials in decorating their shirts. You can decorate the front and back of your shirt with beadwork (see pp. 58-65). Or you can draw a design with a pen and colored ink. However, if designs and symbols are painted on the shirt, it cannot be washed easily.

PLAINS BEADED BUCKSKIN WAR SHIRT

TIE HERE

NECK OPENING AND BEADED FLAP WHICH GOES OVER IT.

HORSE HAIR

TIN

BEADS SEWED TO BUCKSKIN OR CLOTH STRIPS AND THEN SEWED TO SHIRT. USE THE SAME DESIGN FOR ALL STRIPS. STRIPS ARE SEWED TO THE BACK IN SAME POSITION AS IN THE FRONT.

THIS SHIRT CAN BE WORN WITH BUCKSKIN OR DARK CLOTH LEGGINGS WITH WIDE FLAPS OR LONG FRINGE. IT CAN BE WORN LOOSE OR WITH A BEADED BELT.

WOODLAND SHIRT

CHAMOIS SKIN.

TO DYE CLOTH, USE LIGHT BROWN OR ECRU DYE ACCORDING TO DIRECTIONS ON PACKAGE. WRING OUT AS MUCH OF THE RINSE WATER AS POSSIBLE. SHAKE OUT THE CLOTH AND HANG IT UP EVENLY TO DRY. DO NOT IRON IT.

SLIT →

HEAVY OUTING FLANNEL MAKES THE BEST IMITATION BUCKSKIN. NEXT IS UNBLEACHED MUSLIN. USE A LOOSE-FITTING SHIRT FOR YOUR PATTERN.

FOR FRINGE ON CLOTH GARMENTS, BUY CHEAP CHAMOIS SKIN. SEW 3" OR 4" STRIPS TO THE CLOTH AND CUT FRINGE. GET THE CHAMOIS SKIN FIRST AND DYE CLOTH TO MATCH IT. ALLOW ½" ALL AROUND WHEN CUTTING, FOR SEAMS.

BEADED GARTERS WITH LONG FRINGE OF COLORED YARN

BEADED BELT WITH WOODLAND DESIGN

WOODLAND CEREMONIAL SHIRT

WOOL TASSELS

SEWN BEADWORK

APRONS ARE USED FOR BREECH-CLOUTS WITH VELVETEEN SHIRTS.

ALMOST ANY KIND OF BEADS CAN BE USED FOR THESE COSTUMES AS LONG AS THEY ARE UNIFORM IN SIZE. TUBULAR BEADS MAKE NICE BORDERS.

31

CAPES AND YOKES

CAPES and yokes of the type shown on these two pages are worn by the Woodland and some of the Northwestern Indian tribes. They are very effective when worn with a breechclout and leggings and are much cooler for dancing than the war shirt.

The yoke shown on this page can be made of blue, red, or black cloth bound with red or yellow ribbon or binding tape. The back should be beaded in floral designs the same as the front.

The yoke should be backed or lined with other cloth to give it more body; otherwise it will be too flimsy and will not hang right.

The tin-cone spangles are made from pieces of tin cans formed over a nail punch. They should go all the way around the garment for proper effect. Spray them with clear lacquer to keep them from rusting.

The cape at the top of page 33 is made of buckskin and does not have to be lined because

PATTERN
FOR YOKE

32

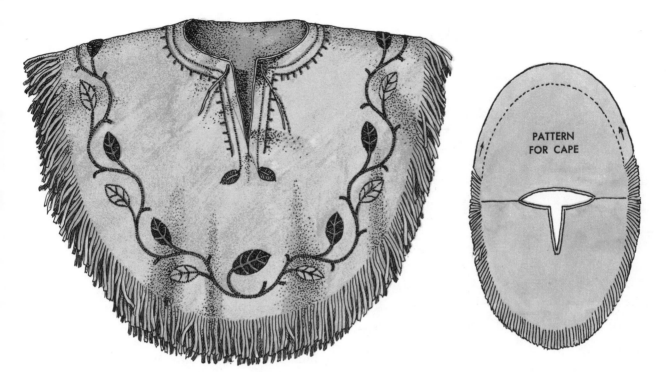

PATTERN
FOR CAPE

it holds its shape very well. It should be fringed all the way around, and the beadwork should continue around the back.

The bearskin cape on this page can be made from an old bearskin rug. Any other dark, straight-hair fur will also do. Sometimes folks have an old fur coat in their attic or basement that you can use.

The outer edge of the cape has a border of bright colored cloth or ribbon.

The bearskin cape is very effective and unusual because it combines the use of bear claws with eagle feathers for decoration. The possession of bear claws and eagle feathers indicated that one was an important member of the tribe.

The bear claws can be whittled out of wood by following the instructions on page 40. The discs are easily made by rounding a clam shell on a grinding wheel and drilling a hole with a steel drill. The eagle feathers should be prepared as shown on page 14.

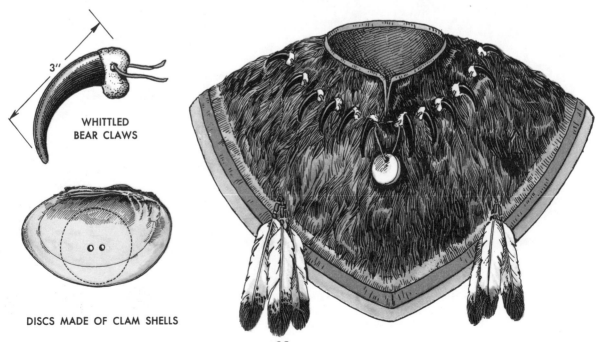

3″

WHITTLED
BEAR CLAWS

DISCS MADE OF CLAM SHELLS

33

VESTS

BEADED vests are comparatively modern. We think that they were copied after the white man's vests. They can be worn with or without a shirt, and add a lot of color to an Indian costume. While not many boys will go to the work of making a fully beaded vest, a partially beaded one on cream-colored leather will be worth the effort. It is better to make a partially beaded vest well than to attempt a completely beaded one and do it poorly. On pages 58-65 you will find directions for beadwork.

Many boys paint designs on their vests with colored airplane cement or dope, scratching through the partially dried cement to represent the rows of beads. I have waited for over half an hour for a ceremonial to end so I could have a good look at an especially attractive beaded vest, only to find that the boy wearing it had painted on the designs with enamel, using the technique shown here.

WOODLAND TYPE

BACK DESIGNS TO MATCH

HALVES OF TWO VESTS WITH FLORAL DESIGNS. IF LEATHER IS THIN, VEST CAN BE LINED WITH BRIGHT COLORED CLOTH. EDGES ARE USUALLY BOUND WITH RIBBON, TO PREVENT LEATHER FROM PULLING OUT OF SHAPE.

34

WESTERN PLAINS TYPE

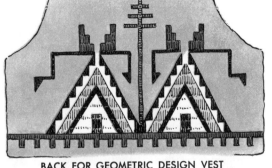

BACK FOR GEOMETRIC DESIGN VEST

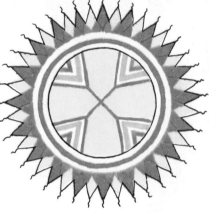

IF YOU PUT HORSES ON THE FRONT, YOU CAN PUT THIS ON THE BACK.

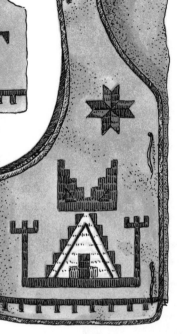

SHOWING TWO DISTINCTIVE TYPES OF SIOUX BEADING. IF YOU USE THE HORSES, HAVE THEM FACING EACH OTHER AND COLOR THEM DIFFERENTLY.

One rarely finds two vests that are alike, so use the illustrations on these two pages for suggestions only. Make your designs original ones so that your vest will be unique.

The best way to start a vest is to make a pattern from your own vest or one that fits you. It does not need to be ripped apart; merely lay it down on a heavy piece of brown wrapping paper and trace a pencil line around it, allowing about ¼ inch wherever there is to be a seam. Then lay the pattern on your vest material, mark its outline, and cut out. These vests should fit rather loosely. If yours is a little bit too big for you, don't worry; you will probably grow into it.

Vests usually are made out of smoked, tanned buckskin. If you cannot get it, any soft leather that has the grain or scarf skin turned to the inside will do. It should be a natural or buckskin color. The edges can be bound with strips of red flannel binding.

If thin buckskin is used, it is advisable to line it with cloth because buckskin sometimes pulls out of shape.

PAINTING

1. LAY OUT THE DESIGN ON THE LEATHER WITH PENCIL.

2. BRUSH A LITTLE CLEAR LACQUER IN THIS AREA, SPREAD AND SMOOTH IT DOWN WITH A FLAT CHISEL-POINTED STICK AND LET IT DRY FOR A FEW MINUTES.

3. PAINT WITH COLORED DOPE OR LACQUER.

4. WHEN IT IS ALMOST DRY SCRATCH LINES THRU THE DOPE ABOUT 1/16" APART WITH A FINE POINTED AWL OR A NEEDLE POINT, TO SIMULATE QUILL WORK. THIS

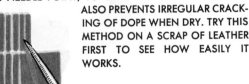

ALSO PREVENTS IRREGULAR CRACKING OF DOPE WHEN DRY. TRY THIS METHOD ON A SCRAP OF LEATHER FIRST TO SEE HOW EASILY IT WORKS.

35

CUFFS AND GAUNTLETS

THE Plains Indians made cuffs and gauntlets which they wore on ceremonial occasions. The Blackfoot especially liked the gauntlet with its large beaded and fringed tops. These were no doubt copied after the riding gauntlets of the United States Cavalry in the Indian territory.

The Sioux, Crow, Ute, and Cheyenne made the cuff part only. These, too, were decorated with bead and quill work. Buckskin is the best material for making gauntlets, but cuffs can be made out of canvas.

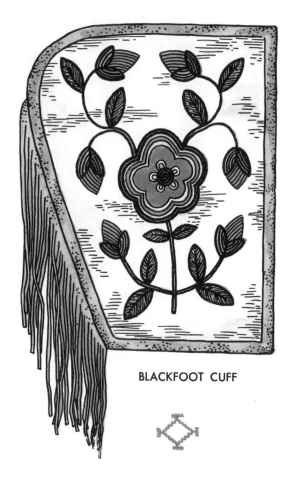

BLACKFOOT CUFF

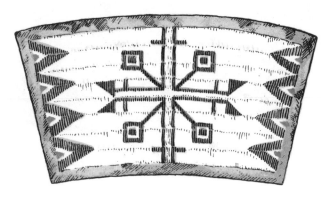

SIOUX CUFF

THESE SIOUX CUFFS WERE BEADED IN LAZY STITCH ON THICK SOFT BUCK-SKIN. LEFT SIDE SHOWS BEADING AND RIGHT SIDE SHOWS PENCIL OUTLINES.

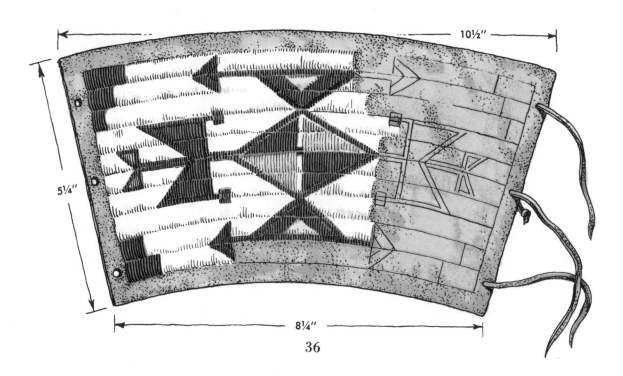

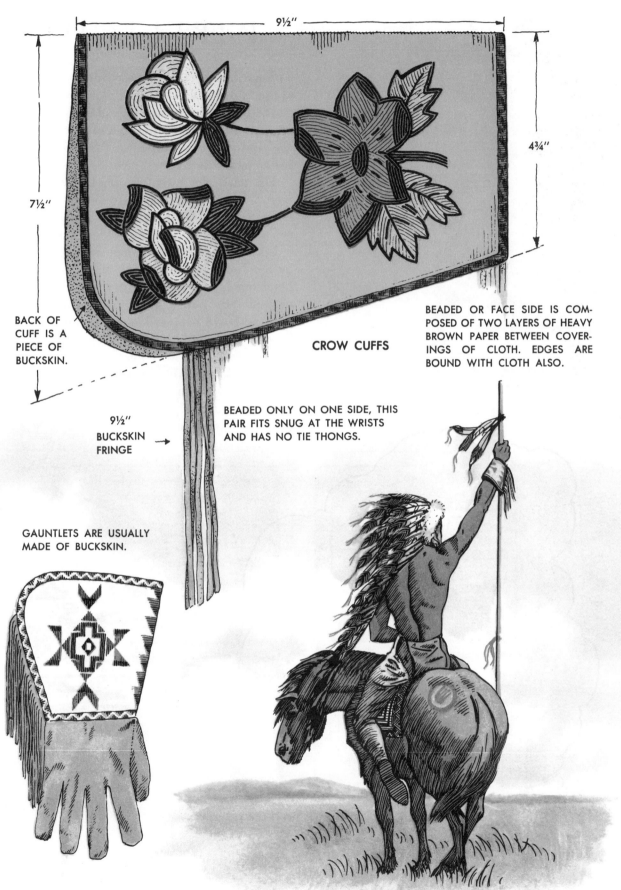

9½"

7½"

4¾"

BACK OF
CUFF IS A
PIECE OF
BUCKSKIN.

BEADED OR FACE SIDE IS COM-
POSED OF TWO LAYERS OF HEAVY
BROWN PAPER BETWEEN COVER-
INGS OF CLOTH. EDGES ARE
BOUND WITH CLOTH ALSO.

CROW CUFFS

9½"
BUCKSKIN
FRINGE

BEADED ONLY ON ONE SIDE, THIS
PAIR FITS SNUG AT THE WRISTS
AND HAS NO TIE THONGS.

GAUNTLETS ARE USUALLY
MADE OF BUCKSKIN.

37

PARFLECHE

THE parfleche is the rawhide skin box or folder of the Plains and Rocky Mountain Indians. The word "parfleche" is of doubtful origin, but was used as early as 1700 to mean rawhide articles. The Indians used parfleches for storing clothing or pemmican (dried meat).

The parfleche is rectangular in shape and is from 2 to 3 feet long. The Indians made it from buffalo rawhide with the hair removed. You can use canvas painted light cream or light gray.

Like most of the other ordinary articles used by the Indians in daily life, the parfleche was handsomely decorated. Paint yours with enamel or ordinary house paint, using one of the designs shown below. The usual colors are red, black, yellow and green.

The parfleche shown here will take an entire outfit—full war shirt, buckskin leggings, necklace, moccasins, and even a war bonnet. After packing your equipment in the parfleche, tie it shut with the thongs, and hang it up.

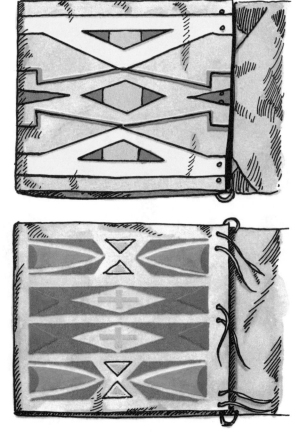

38

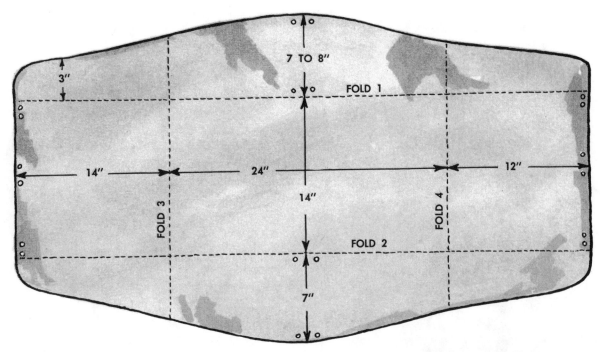

CUT PARFLECHE AS SHOWN ABOVE. PAINT THE OUTSIDE LIGHT CREAM OR GRAY. LET DRY THOROUGHLY. THEN DECORATE FRONT FLAPS WITH DESIGNS. FINALLY PUNCH HOLES SHOWN ABOVE.

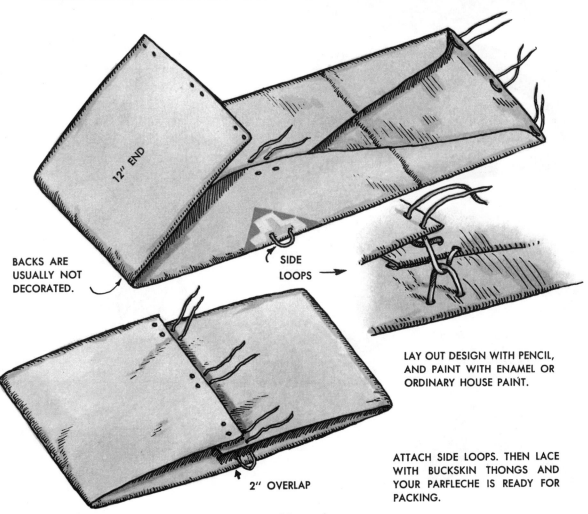

BACKS ARE USUALLY NOT DECORATED.

SIDE LOOPS

2" OVERLAP

LAY OUT DESIGN WITH PENCIL, AND PAINT WITH ENAMEL OR ORDINARY HOUSE PAINT.

ATTACH SIDE LOOPS. THEN LACE WITH BUCKSKIN THONGS AND YOUR PARFLECHE IS READY FOR PACKING.

BEAR CLAW NECKLACE

PUT ON NECKLACE TO SEE HOW MANY BEADS TO STRING BETWEEN CLAWS.

CUT FUR PIECES TO FOLD OVER NECKLACE BETWEEN CLAWS. A DROP OF CEMENT WILL HELP.

INDIANS made necklaces out of practically anything that took their fancy. Eagle and grizzly bear claws were prized by them because it required much skill and daring to get them. Because of the shortage of grizzly bears these days, you can carve a set of claws out of wood that will deceive even an old Indian. Use bass, gum or white pine. To give the wooden claws a natural color, follow the directions below. String the claws on a double buckskin thong. Use beads or pieces of fur to separate the claws.

1. SAW OUT THE BLANKS. BLOCK OUT THE ROUGH SHAPES.

LIGHTEN UPPER PART WITH FINE SAND-PAPER. POLISH CLAW WITH CLOTH.

4. RUN CLAW THROUGH THE PARAFFIN NOW AND THEN. KEEP THIS UP UNTIL IT AC-QUIRES A HORN-LIKE AP-PEARANCE.

2. WHITTLE AND SANDPAPER INTO FINISHED FORM. PAINT BASE RED BEFORE COLORING CLAW. PAINT WILL NOT STICK TO A WAXED SURFACE.

3. HOLD CLAW OVER CANDLE FLAME TO DARKEN IT. DON'T CHAR IT TOO MUCH.

40

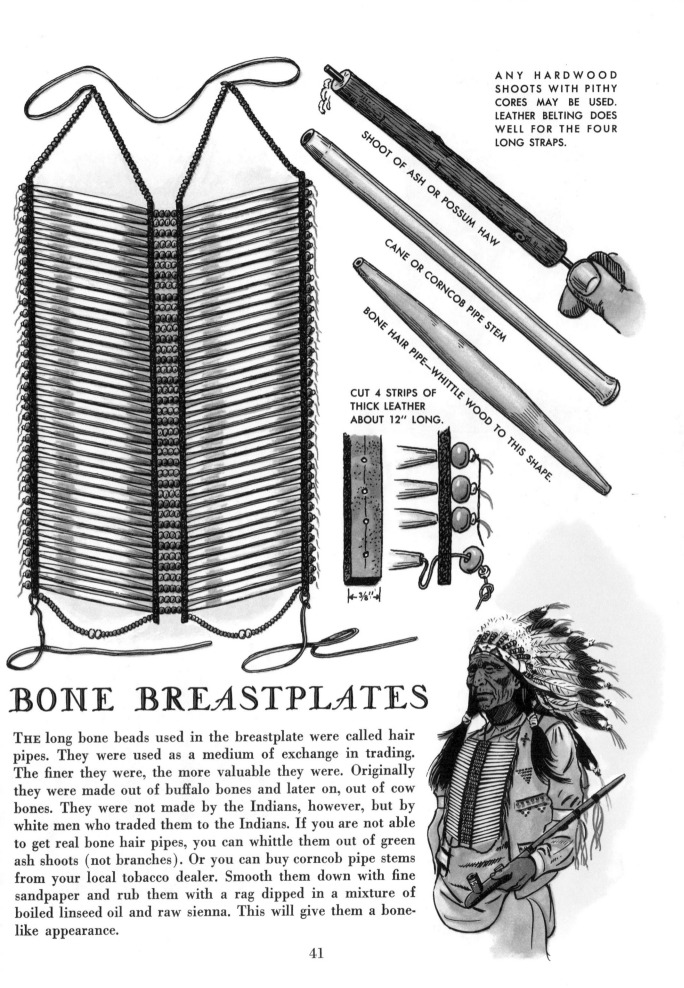

ANY HARDWOOD
SHOOTS WITH PITHY
CORES MAY BE USED.
LEATHER BELTING DOES
WELL FOR THE FOUR
LONG STRAPS.

SHOOT OF ASH OR POSSUM HAW

CANE OR CORNCOB PIPE STEM

BONE HAIR PIPE—WHITTLE WOOD TO THIS SHAPE.

CUT 4 STRIPS OF
THICK LEATHER
ABOUT 12" LONG.

|← 3/8" →|

BONE BREASTPLATES

THE long bone beads used in the breastplate were called hair
pipes. They were used as a medium of exchange in trading.
The finer they were, the more valuable they were. Originally
they were made out of buffalo bones and later on, out of cow
bones. They were not made by the Indians, however, but by
white men who traded them to the Indians. If you are not able
to get real bone hair pipes, you can whittle them out of green
ash shoots (not branches). Or you can buy corncob pipe stems
from your local tobacco dealer. Smooth them down with fine
sandpaper and rub them with a rag dipped in a mixture of
boiled linseed oil and raw sienna. This will give them a bone-
like appearance.

41

CHOKERS AND TIES

THE choker is a band that fastens about the neck. The tie is the choker plus a strip hanging down from it. It is much the same as the white man's necktie.

Chokers and ties are a rather modern addition to the Indian costume and look equally well whether worn with or without a shirt.

These two decorations are usually beaded with the lazy squaw style of beadwork stitch. However, the choker can be beaded on a loom if it is to be worn without a tie. Pendants are then suspended from it. These pendants should

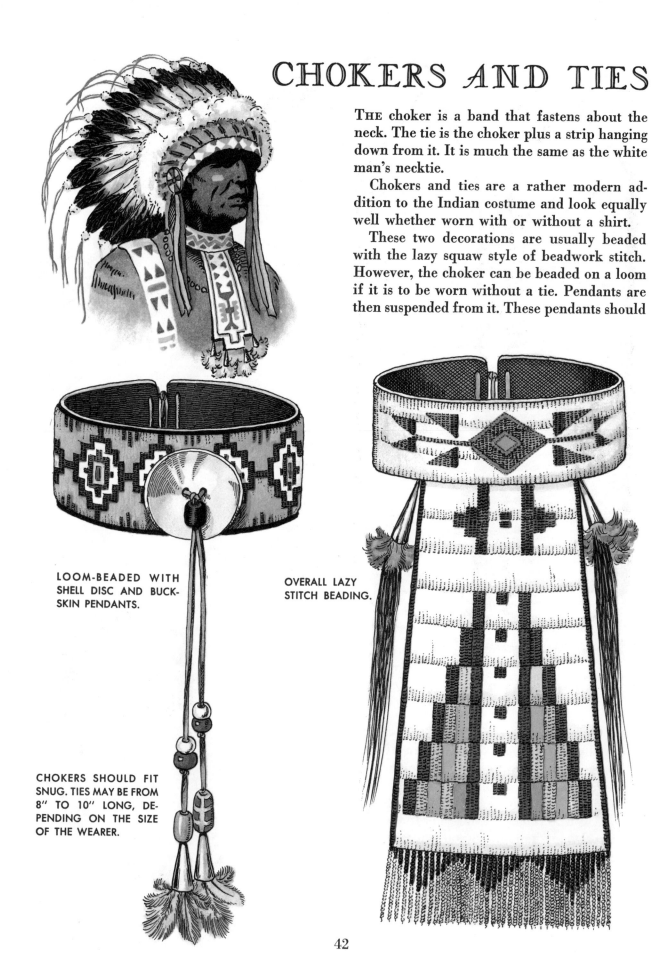

LOOM-BEADED WITH SHELL DISC AND BUCK-SKIN PENDANTS.

OVERALL LAZY STITCH BEADING.

CHOKERS SHOULD FIT SNUG. TIES MAY BE FROM 8" TO 10" LONG, DE-PENDING ON THE SIZE OF THE WEARER.

42

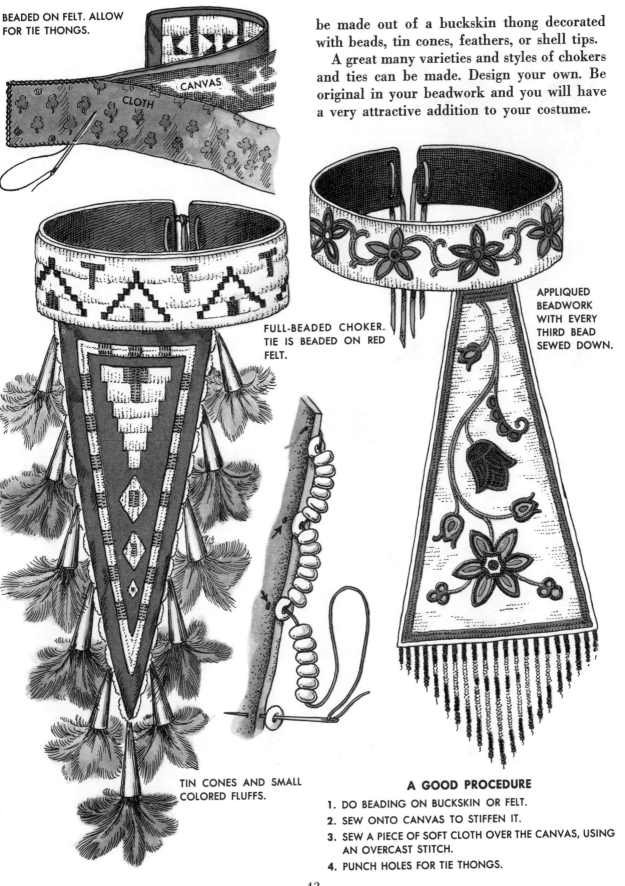

BEADED ON FELT. ALLOW FOR TIE THONGS.

CANVAS

CLOTH

be made out of a buckskin thong decorated with beads, tin cones, feathers, or shell tips.

A great many varieties and styles of chokers and ties can be made. Design your own. Be original in your beadwork and you will have a very attractive addition to your costume.

APPLIQUED BEADWORK WITH EVERY THIRD BEAD SEWED DOWN.

FULL-BEADED CHOKER. TIE IS BEADED ON RED FELT.

TIN CONES AND SMALL COLORED FLUFFS.

A GOOD PROCEDURE

1. DO BEADING ON BUCKSKIN OR FELT.
2. SEW ONTO CANVAS TO STIFFEN IT.
3. SEW A PIECE OF SOFT CLOTH OVER THE CANVAS, USING AN OVERCAST STITCH.
4. PUNCH HOLES FOR TIE THONGS.

MOCCASINS

fallen trees, and walking along ledges. Their boots became heavy when wet, and refused to dry out over night; and, after getting wet and drying out a few times, the leather cracked open. The pioneers soon found that the soft moccasin worn by the Indian was ideal.

The name for the soft skin shoe of the North American Indian is derived from the Eastern Algonquin dialect "Mockasin" or "Mawhca-sun." With the exception of some of the Indians living along the Mexican boundary, Southern Plains, and the Northwest Coast, who generally went barefooted, the moccasin was almost universally worn.

There are two general types of moccasins. The first has a rawhide sole sewed to a soft-leather upper, and the second is made with the sole and the upper part from one piece of soft leather, with the seam being at the instep and heel. The hard-soled moccasin belonged to the Plains tribes, protecting their feet from the rough stones and cactus. The Plains and the Southwest Indians had the thick rawhide from the buffalo available for their hard-soled moccasins. The soft-soled moccasin belonged to the Woodland tribes, being adaptable to woodland travel and canoe use.

WHEN the explorer and the settler started to invade the forests, mountains, and streams of the Indian, they soon found that their hard-soled, heavy boot was not a suitable type of footwear for crawling over slippery rocks and

THE PATTERN IS IMPORTANT. LAY IT OUT CAREFULLY AND CUT THE LEATHER CAREFULLY.

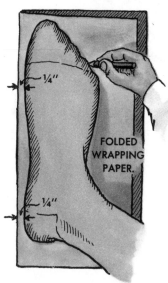

1. PLACE FOOT ¼" FROM FOLDED EDGE OF PAPER AND MARK OUTLINE OF FOOT.

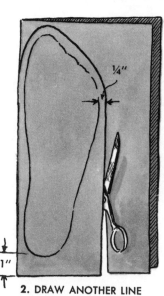

DO YOUR CUTTING WITH SHARP SHEARS.

2. DRAW ANOTHER LINE ¼" FROM OUTLINE OF FOOT AS SHOWN ABOVE. CUT ALONG THIS LINE.

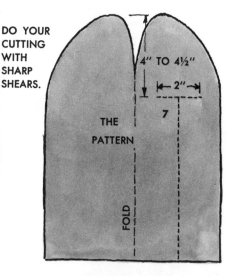

THE PATTERN

3. LAY PATTERN FLAT ON LEATHER. CUT OUT TWO VERY CAREFULLY. DON'T CUT AT DOTTED LINES UNTIL STEP 7.

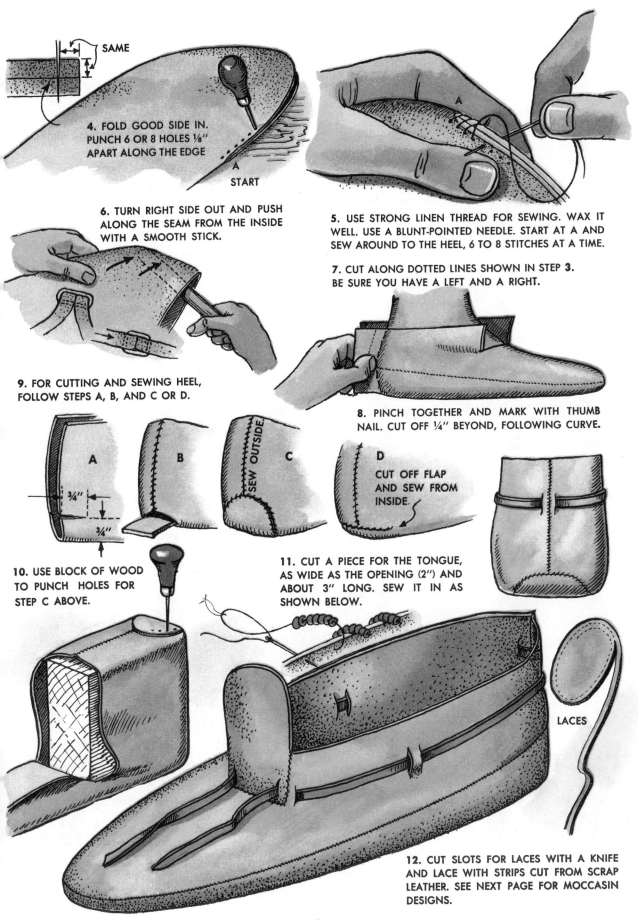

SAME

4. FOLD GOOD SIDE IN. PUNCH 6 OR 8 HOLES ⅛" APART ALONG THE EDGE

START

6. TURN RIGHT SIDE OUT AND PUSH ALONG THE SEAM FROM THE INSIDE WITH A SMOOTH STICK.

5. USE STRONG LINEN THREAD FOR SEWING. WAX IT WELL. USE A BLUNT-POINTED NEEDLE. START AT A AND SEW AROUND TO THE HEEL, 6 TO 8 STITCHES AT A TIME.

7. CUT ALONG DOTTED LINES SHOWN IN STEP **3**. BE SURE YOU HAVE A LEFT AND A RIGHT.

9. FOR CUTTING AND SEWING HEEL, FOLLOW STEPS A, B, AND C OR D.

8. PINCH TOGETHER AND MARK WITH THUMB NAIL. CUT OFF ¼" BEYOND, FOLLOWING CURVE.

A

¾"

¾"

B

SEW OUTSIDE.

C

D

CUT OFF FLAP AND SEW FROM INSIDE.

10. USE BLOCK OF WOOD TO PUNCH HOLES FOR STEP C ABOVE.

11. CUT A PIECE FOR THE TONGUE, AS WIDE AS THE OPENING (2") AND ABOUT 3" LONG. SEW IT IN AS SHOWN BELOW.

LACES

12. CUT SLOTS FOR LACES WITH A KNIFE AND LACE WITH STRIPS CUT FROM SCRAP LEATHER. SEE NEXT PAGE FOR MOCCASIN DESIGNS.

MOCCASINS (Continued)

There were many designs and patterns. The Chippewa (Ojibwa) make moccasins with a puckered seam. Their name is said to mean "roast till puckered up," referring to their moccasins.

Each tribe made and decorated their moccasins in a little different way. An Indian Scout in the old days could tell, from a discarded moccasin along the trail, what tribe had passed that way. Some of the Indians on a war party wore the moccasins of other tribes to confuse the enemy scouts.

The moccasins I have found to be easiest for boys to make are the Nez Perce type, with Ute tongues. This type has the seam running along the side of the foot from the great toe to the heel.

This moccasin, made out of split cowhide, called glove splits, and carefully sewed with a good linen thread, thoroughly waxed, will last an entire camping season. Ask your leather dealer for medium weight, soft skins. This leather comes in several colors—pearl gray, yellow and terra cotta (brick red). A half hide will make three to six pairs, depending on the size of the hide.

I would like to point out that the sewing must be done slowly, carefully and evenly, so that when the moccasin is turned right side out, no large or uneven stitches will be seen.

While you are cutting the skins, plan on making several pairs. The Indian always took two pairs of moccasins on his trips, because when one became wet or worn out, he always had a second pair handy.

Decorate your moccasins to conform with the type of design used by the tribe you are portraying. Originally, moccasins were stained with earth colors or decorated with quill work. Later on, when the white man traded beads to the Indians, quill work gave way to beadwork designs. You can decorate your moccasins with either painting or beadwork quite easily. The Plains Indians decorated their moccasins with not less than three different colors of quills. Their favorites were yellow, red, green and purple.

Beaded moccasins had a larger range of colors, the average being four or five, and the preference was white, red, green, yellow and blue. The background color, almost exclusively, was white, although the Assiniboin tribe used blue for the background color. Today the Chippewa are embroidering their moccasins with bright colored yarn.

WOODLAND DESIGNS

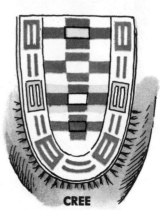

IROQUOIS
BEADED ON CANVAS AND SEWED ONTO BUCKSKIN.

CHIPPEWA
BEADED ON BLACK VELVETEEN.

CREE
BEADED ON SEPARATE PIECE OF BUCKSKIN.

CHIPEWYAN

EMBROIDERED WITH
YARN ON BLACK
FLANNEL. (MODERN)

ALGONQUIN

BEADED DIRECTLY ON
MOCCASIN.

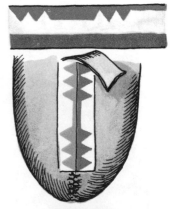

WINNEBAGO

BEADED OVER
PUCKERING.

WESTERN AND PLAINS DESIGNS

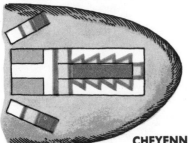

CHEYENNE

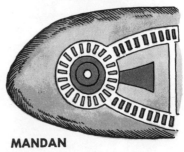

MANDAN

BLACKFOOT

SIOUX

QUILL WORK AND BEADED BORDER

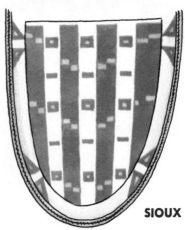

SIOUX

ARAPAHO

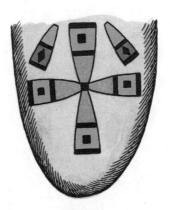

CROW

CROW

47

ARM BANDS AND ANKLETS

ARM BANDS may be worn on the bare arm between the shoulder and the elbow. Or they may be worn over the shirt sleeve of your Indian costume.

Plain bands can be made from stainless steel, brass, or 14-gauge aluminum. They should be brightly polished. If you spray them with clear lacquer after polishing, they will stay shiny for a long time.

Beaded arm bands can be made of thin rawhide or thin leather. They should be about 2½ inches wide, or narrower. They should not completely encircle the arm, so that when you tie the leather thongs they will fit snugly and will not slip down.

A band of thin rawhide or leather, to which sleigh bells are attached, can also be used for anklets. The bells can be obtained in a hardware store or in the toy section of a department store. These bands can be worn either fastened tightly below the knee, or loosely around the ankle.

ARM BANDS

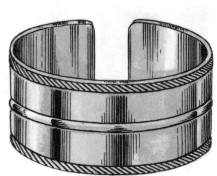

THE SIMPLEST ARM BANDS ARE MADE OF STAINLESS STEEL OR BRASS. MAKE THEM 2" TO 3" WIDE AND 8" TO 10" LONG, DEPENDING ON SIZE OF ARM. ALUMINUM CAN EASILY BE STAMPED.

COLORFUL ARM BANDS CAN BE MADE OF ¼" TUBULAR BEADS ON A LOOM. USE WAXED CORD INSTEAD OF THREAD. THESE ARE EASY FOR BEGINNERS TO MAKE.

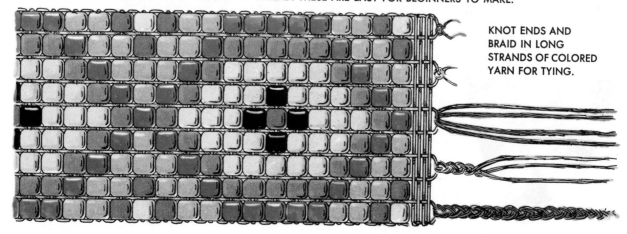

KNOT ENDS AND BRAID IN LONG STRANDS OF COLORED YARN FOR TYING.

CONVENTIONAL TYPES OF BANDS ARE EITHER LOOM BEADED OR LAZY STITCHED AND SHOULD BE SEWED ONTO A FIRM CANVAS OR LEATHER BASE.

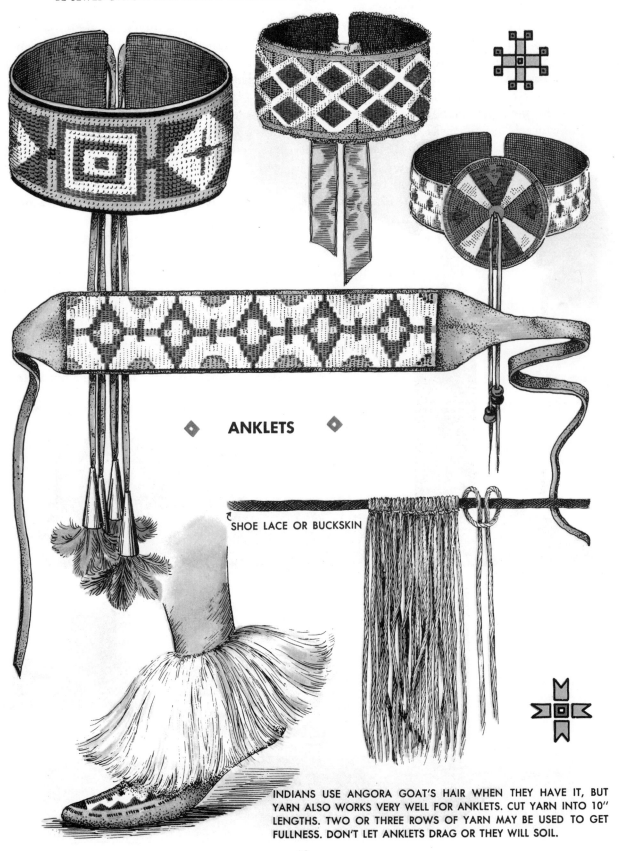

◆ **ANKLETS** ◆

SHOE LACE OR BUCKSKIN

INDIANS USE ANGORA GOAT'S HAIR WHEN THEY HAVE IT, BUT YARN ALSO WORKS VERY WELL FOR ANKLETS. CUT YARN INTO 10" LENGTHS. TWO OR THREE ROWS OF YARN MAY BE USED TO GET FULLNESS. DON'T LET ANKLETS DRAG OR THEY WILL SOIL.

PEACE PIPES

THE use of the peace pipe was held sacred by the Indians. Usually it was used in ceremonies of religious, political, or social nature. The decorations on the pipe's bowl and stem, and even the method of holding or passing the pipe on to the next person, held great ceremonial significance. The pipe was never laid on the ground. To smoke it was a signal that the smoker gave his pledge of honor. It was also believed that the smoke made one think clearly and endowed him with great wisdom. In a treaty ceremony, the pipe usually was passed around to everyone, even before the speeches were made and the problems discussed.

Some pipes were made out of wood, clay, or bone. But the most popular and the most treasured were those made of the soft catlinite mined in the pipestone quarries of Minnesota.

These red stone quarries were considered sacred by the Dakotas (Sioux), and were traditionally neutral ground for all tribes. Indians traveled many miles to get this pipestone, and it was a medium of barter between various tribes. The stone was so soft that it could be cut and worked into designs with a knife when freshly quarried. Some pipes were inlaid with lead. It is said that some of the Indian raids on small western town newspapers were made by the Indians to get type lead with which to inlay their pipes.

A very effective pipe can be made out of wood. It probably will be much more practical for your Indian ceremonials since it will not break. Sumac and ash are good woods to use for the stem because they are easy to whittle. The stem can be decorated with feathers, horse hair, plumes, or colored cloth. If you want to make a pipe that will really work, you can drill a hole through the stem by using a hot wire.

IF THE PIPE IS NOT TO BE SMOKED, DRILL ONLY FOR THE STEM AND TOBACCO HOLES. PIPESTEMS CAN THEN BE A SOLID PIECE ALSO.

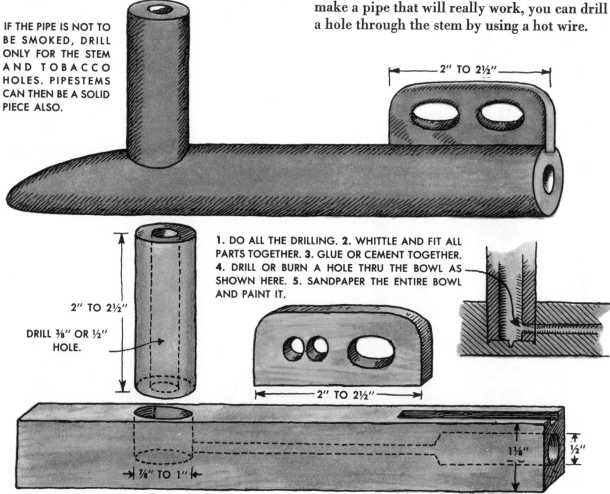

2" TO 2½"

2" TO 2½"

DRILL ⅜" OR ½" HOLE.

1. DO ALL THE DRILLING. 2. WHITTLE AND FIT ALL PARTS TOGETHER. 3. GLUE OR CEMENT TOGETHER. 4. DRILL OR BURN A HOLE THRU THE BOWL AS SHOWN HERE. 5. SANDPAPER THE ENTIRE BOWL AND PAINT IT.

2" TO 2½"

1⅛"   ½"

⅞" TO 1"

DECORATE PEACE PIPE WITH
FEATHERS, FUR, AND HORSEHAIR
OR WITH WRAPPED BEADWORK.

ALMOST ANY PEACE PIPE SHOWN IN BOOKS OR
IN MUSEUMS CAN BE COPIED IN WOOD.

DRILL MADE FROM A PIECE OF HEAVY WIRE
WITH THE END FLATTENED AND FILED.

SUMAC IS A GOOD WOOD
TO USE BECAUSE IT IS
EASY TO WHITTLE.

INLAYING PIPE BOWLS

INLAID PIPE BOWLS ARE FAIRLY MODERN. INDIANS
INLAID THEM WITH LEAD, TYPE METAL, OR PEW-
TER. SOME SAY IT WAS DONE TO REINFORCE THE
STONE AND SOME SAY IT WAS FOR ORNAMEN-
TATION ONLY.

YOU CAN DO A FAIRLY GOOD IMITATION INLAY JOB WITH ALUMINUM PAINT. FIRST PAINT THE ENTIRE PIPE BOWL
WITH FLAT BRICK-RED PAINT AND ALLOW IT TO DRY. THEN LAY OUT THE "INLAY" AND PAINT IT CAREFULLY WITH A
SMALL BRUSH. A COAT OF WAX OR FLAT VARNISH OVER ALL WILL FINISH IT UP VERY REALISTICALLY.

51

BAGS AND POUCHES

BAGS and pouches were used by all Indian tribes for many purposes. Bags were larger than pouches and usually were decorated with quill or beadwork. They were used to carry pipes, food, fire-making equipment, and miscellaneous objects. Pouches were smaller decorated containers used for carrying medicine, tobacco, sewing tools, and other personal articles.

You will need a bag and several pouches for your peace pipe, pocket knife, money, and other property because your breechclout and leggings do not have any pockets.

KNOT ENDS OF THONGS TO FASTEN TIN CONES.

OPEN TOP POUCH

BACK   OPEN

4½" BEADED BELT POUCH

BUCKSKIN AND CANVAS

ONLY FRONT IS BEADED.

14" UTE PIPE BAG

POUCH

PENDANT

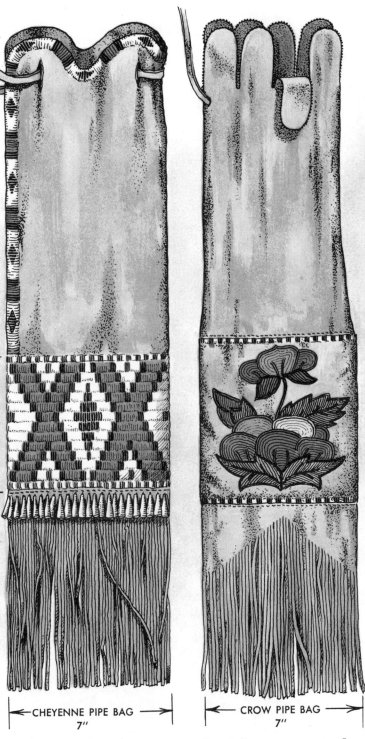

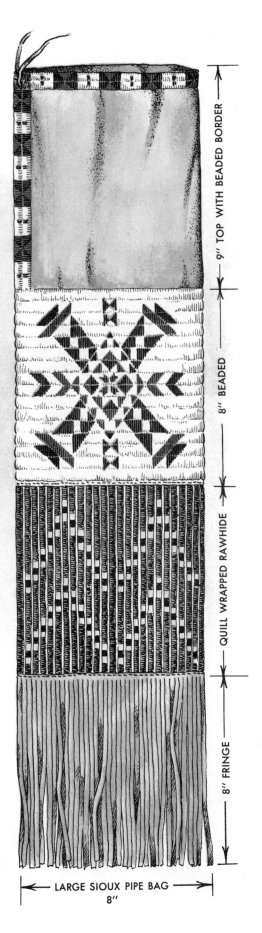

Most of the larger bags are made of three parts sewed together: top, beaded section, and fringe. Decorate them with original designs of the tribe that you are portraying. A good imitation of porcupine quill wrapping can be done by painting ¼" strips of leather with airplane dope. (See page 61.) Bags can be tucked over or under the belt, and pouches can be either fastened to the belt or carried inside the bags.

53

SUNBURST BUSTLES

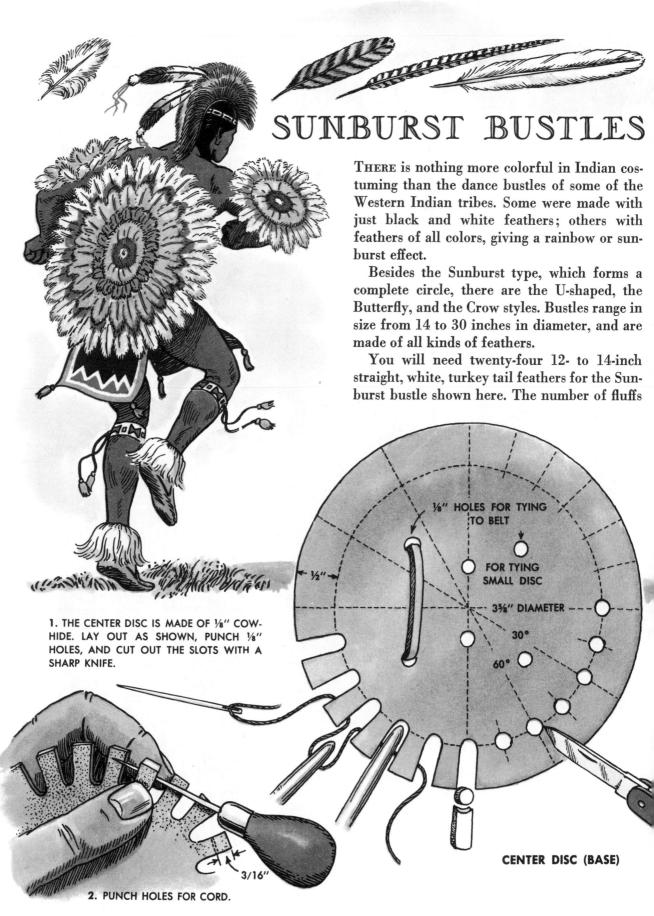

THERE is nothing more colorful in Indian costuming than the dance bustles of some of the Western Indian tribes. Some were made with just black and white feathers; others with feathers of all colors, giving a rainbow or sunburst effect.

Besides the Sunburst type, which forms a complete circle, there are the U-shaped, the Butterfly, and the Crow styles. Bustles range in size from 14 to 30 inches in diameter, and are made of all kinds of feathers.

You will need twenty-four 12- to 14-inch straight, white, turkey tail feathers for the Sunburst bustle shown here. The number of fluffs

⅛" HOLES FOR TYING TO BELT

FOR TYING SMALL DISC

½"

3⅝" DIAMETER

30°

60°

1. THE CENTER DISC IS MADE OF ⅛" COWHIDE. LAY OUT AS SHOWN, PUNCH ⅛" HOLES, AND CUT OUT THE SLOTS WITH A SHARP KNIFE.

CENTER DISC (BASE)

2. PUNCH HOLES FOR CORD.

3/16"

54

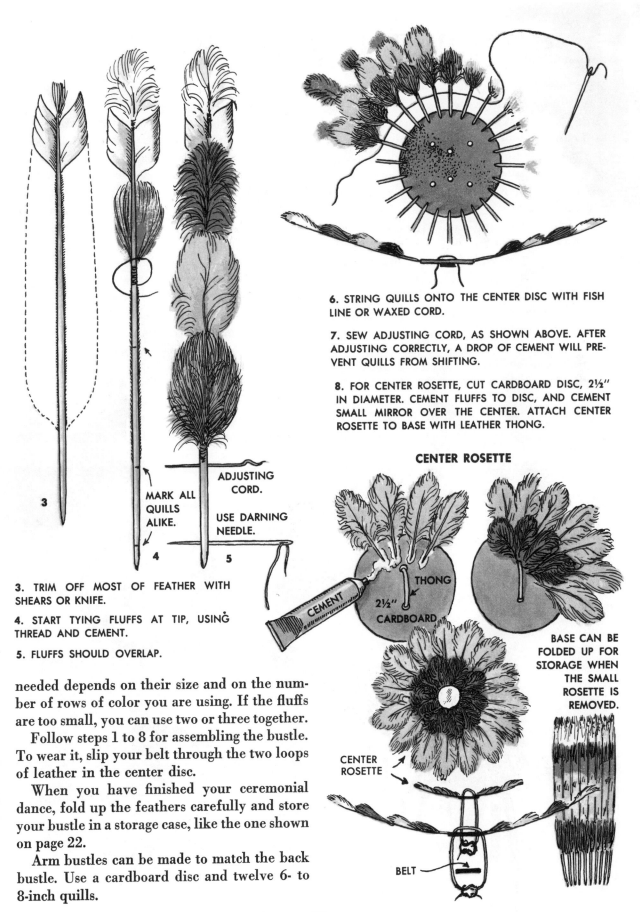

6. STRING QUILLS ONTO THE CENTER DISC WITH FISH LINE OR WAXED CORD.

7. SEW ADJUSTING CORD, AS SHOWN ABOVE. AFTER ADJUSTING CORRECTLY, A DROP OF CEMENT WILL PREVENT QUILLS FROM SHIFTING.

8. FOR CENTER ROSETTE, CUT CARDBOARD DISC, 2½" IN DIAMETER. CEMENT FLUFFS TO DISC, AND CEMENT SMALL MIRROR OVER THE CENTER. ATTACH CENTER ROSETTE TO BASE WITH LEATHER THONG.

CENTER ROSETTE

THONG

CEMENT

2½" CARDBOARD

BASE CAN BE FOLDED UP FOR STORAGE WHEN THE SMALL ROSETTE IS REMOVED.

CENTER ROSETTE

BELT

MARK ALL QUILLS ALIKE.

ADJUSTING CORD.

USE DARNING NEEDLE.

3   4   5

3. TRIM OFF MOST OF FEATHER WITH SHEARS OR KNIFE.

4. START TYING FLUFFS AT TIP, USING THREAD AND CEMENT.

5. FLUFFS SHOULD OVERLAP.

needed depends on their size and on the number of rows of color you are using. If the fluffs are too small, you can use two or three together.

Follow steps 1 to 8 for assembling the bustle. To wear it, slip your belt through the two loops of leather in the center disc.

When you have finished your ceremonial dance, fold up the feathers carefully and store your bustle in a storage case, like the one shown on page 22.

Arm bustles can be made to match the back bustle. Use a cardboard disc and twelve 6- to 8-inch quills.

CHIPPEWA MIDE BUSTLE

This bustle was sketched from one worn by a Chippewa Medicine Man, Go-go-we-osh (Frank Smart). It was made of black velveteen, but it can also be made of red or blue cloth. If it is made of a light-weight material, it should be lined so it will hang right. The feathers are prepared with loops and fluffs just as they are for a war bonnet.

The Midewiwin or Grand Medicine Society of the Ojibwa Indians was a very powerful organization. The rites were celebrated in a grand medicine lodge called the "midewiga-mig." This long wigwam was built of birchbark over a framework of saplings, from 100 to 200 feet long. The top was open, but could be closed during bad weather with mats made of cattails and birchbark sewed together.

Near the medicine lodge was a small lodge about 10 feet in diameter and about 6 feet high, with an opening at the top. This lodge was also built of bent saplings which were covered with birchbark. It served a special ceremonial purpose during the Midewiwin ceremonials, as a sweat lodge.

The ceremonies of the Midewiwin are carefully observed even today, but anyone outside the tribe has very little information about its activities.

The traditional history of the Ojibwa tribe, the long prayers, speeches, and songs are preserved on birchbark charts called "Midé Rolls." These rolls of birchbark are illustrated with symbolic drawings, and are used to prompt the performers as they take part in the long ceremonies.

The ceremonial meetings of the Midewiwin were held once a year, and candidates were initiated into the Society by Mide priests commonly called "Medicine Men." It was considered a great honor to be admitted to the Society, and membership was difficult to obtain.

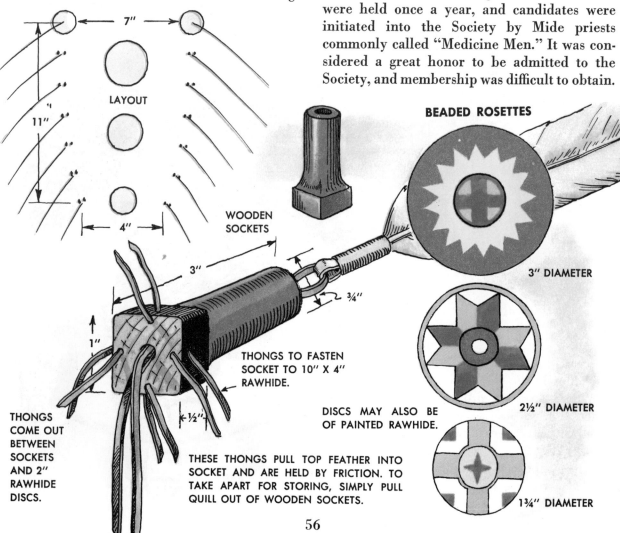

LAYOUT

7"

11"

4"

WOODEN SOCKETS

BEADED ROSETTES

3" DIAMETER

2½" DIAMETER

1¾" DIAMETER

3"

¾"

1"

½"

THONGS TO FASTEN SOCKET TO 10" X 4" RAWHIDE.

THONGS COME OUT BETWEEN SOCKETS AND 2" RAWHIDE DISCS.

THESE THONGS PULL TOP FEATHER INTO SOCKET AND ARE HELD BY FRICTION. TO TAKE APART FOR STORING, SIMPLY PULL QUILL OUT OF WOODEN SOCKETS.

DISCS MAY ALSO BE OF PAINTED RAWHIDE.

56

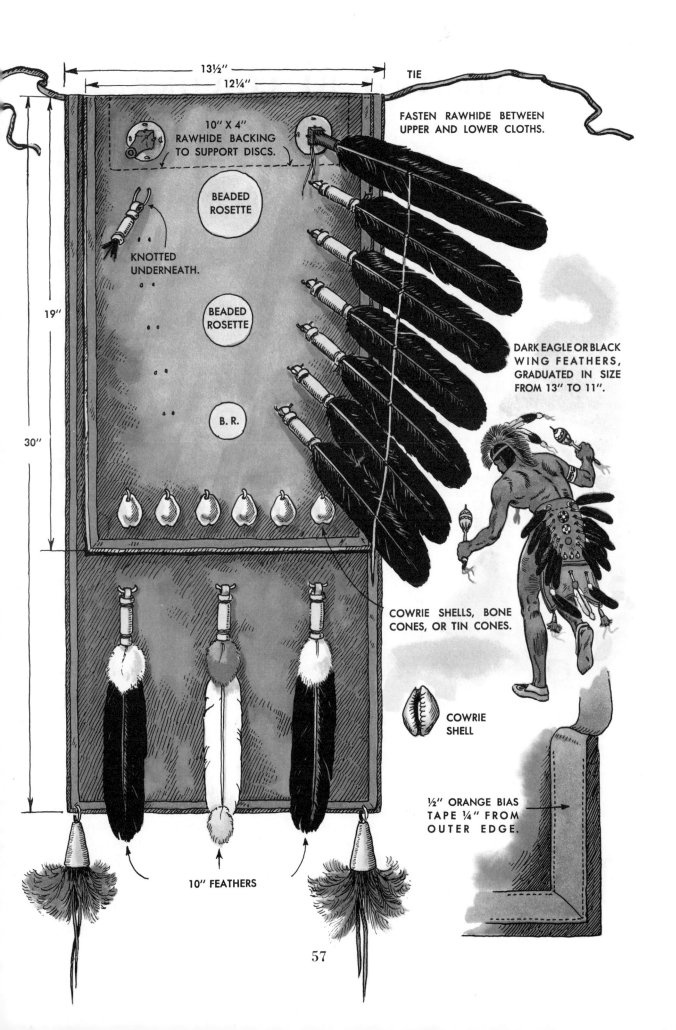

13½"

12¼"

TIE

FASTEN RAWHIDE BETWEEN
UPPER AND LOWER CLOTHS.

10" X 4"
RAWHIDE BACKING
TO SUPPORT DISCS.

BEADED
ROSETTE

KNOTTED
UNDERNEATH.

BEADED
ROSETTE

19"

B. R.

DARK EAGLE OR BLACK
WING FEATHERS,
GRADUATED IN SIZE
FROM 13" TO 11".

30"

COWRIE SHELLS, BONE
CONES, OR TIN CONES.

COWRIE
SHELL

½" ORANGE BIAS
TAPE ¼" FROM
OUTER EDGE.

10" FEATHERS

57

INDIAN BEADWORK

By the time Columbus discovered America, the Indians were already using beads for decoration. Beads were made from shells, bones, claws, stones, and minerals.

The Algonquin and Iroquois tribes of the eastern coast made beads from clam, conch, periwinkle, and other seashells. These beads were used as a medium of exchange by the early Dutch and English colonists. They were called "wampum," a contraction of the Algonquin "wampumpeak" or "wamponeage," meaning string of shell beads. The purple beads had twice the value of the white ones.

The explorer, followed by the trader, missionary and settler, soon discovered that he had a very good trade item in glass beads brought from Europe.

The early beads that were used were about ⅛ inch in diameter, nearly twice as large as beads in the mid-1800's. They were called pony beads and were quite irregular in shape and size. The colors most commonly used were sky-blue, white, and black. Other less widely used colors were deep buff, light red, dark red, and dark blue.

The small, round seed beads, as they are called, are the most generally used for sewed beadwork. They come in a variety of colors. Those most commonly used by the Indians are red, orange, yellow, light blue, dark blue, green, lavender, and black.

The missionaries' floral embroidered vestments influenced the Woodland tribes of the Great Lakes to apply beads in flower designs. Many other tribes, however, are now using flower designs. There are four main design styles used in the modern period. Three of the styles are largely restricted to particular tribes. The fourth style is common to all groups. It is very simple in pattern. The motifs generally used are solid triangles, hourglasses, crosses, and oblongs. This style is usually used in narrow strips on leggings, robes, or blankets.

Sioux beadwork usually is quite open with a solid background in a light color. White is used almost exclusively, although medium or light blue is sometimes seen. The design colors are dominated by red and blue with yellow and green used sparingly. The lazy stitch is used as an application.

The Crow and Shoshoni usually beaded on red trade or blanket cloth, using the cloth itself for a background. White was rarely used, except as a thin line outlining other design elements. The most common colors used for designs are pale lavender, pale blue, green, and yellow. On rare occasions, dark blue was used. Red beads were not used very often because they blended with the background color of the cloth and could not be seen. The applique stitch was used.

Blackfoot beadwork can be identified by the myriad of little squares or oblongs massed together to make up a larger unit of design such as triangles, squares, diamonds, terraces, and crosses. The large figure is usually of one color and the little units edging it of many colors. The background color is usually white, although other light colors such as light blue and green have been used.

The smallness of the pattern in Blackfoot designs would indicate this style is quite modern, as pony trading beads would be too large to work into these designs.

Beadwork made in this style seems to imitate the designs of the woven quill work of some of the northwestern tribes with whom the Blackfoot came in contact. The applique stitch is used exclusively for application.

There are three types of beadwork generally used for Indian lore beading—the loom type, the lazy or lazy squaw stitch, and the applique stitch.

Loom beading is the most popular because

PONY BEADS   SEED BEADS

INDIAN-MADE   WAMPUM MADE BY
WAMPUM   WHITE MEN

LOOM BEADING

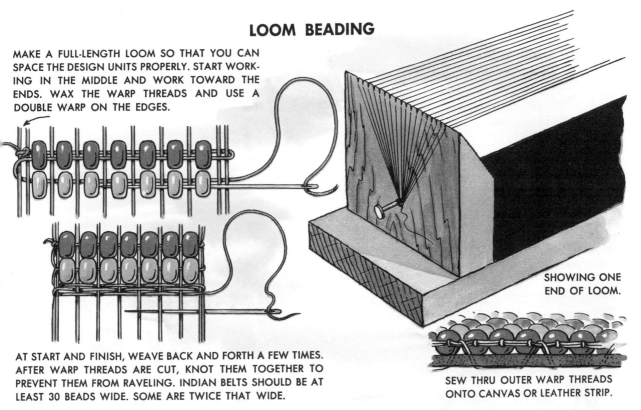

MAKE A FULL-LENGTH LOOM SO THAT YOU CAN SPACE THE DESIGN UNITS PROPERLY. START WORKING IN THE MIDDLE AND WORK TOWARD THE ENDS. WAX THE WARP THREADS AND USE A DOUBLE WARP ON THE EDGES.

SHOWING ONE END OF LOOM.

AT START AND FINISH, WEAVE BACK AND FORTH A FEW TIMES. AFTER WARP THREADS ARE CUT, KNOT THEM TOGETHER TO PREVENT THEM FROM RAVELING. INDIAN BELTS SHOULD BE AT LEAST 30 BEADS WIDE. SOME ARE TWICE THAT WIDE.

SEW THRU OUTER WARP THREADS ONTO CANVAS OR LEATHER STRIP.

it is somewhat easier to do. Belts, hat bands, and leggings strips can be easily beaded in this manner. To do this type of beading you must first make yourself a loom. (See picture.)

The loom should be about $2\frac{1}{4}$ inches wide and about 6 inches longer than your longest beaded object will be. The knife cuts that will hold the warp threads should be about 1/16 inch deep and about $\frac{1}{8}$ inch apart for easy weaving. Paint the loom with dull black paint to eliminate as much eye strain as possible, because beading is very close work.

To begin work, the loom should be threaded with the warp threads. Each thread should be fitted in the groove and the ends tied to the screws on the end boards. Usually a loom is threaded with an even number of warp threads. This will give you an uneven number of beads in your finished beadwork.

The warp threads should be heavier than the weft threads. No. 60 linen thread is best for the weft. All threads should be well waxed with beeswax to preserve them and to keep the beads from shifting.

It is very important that the beads used in loom beading should be uniform in size. Loom beading made with run-of-the-mill beads will look very rough and patched.

LAZY STITCH BEADING

SEW ONTO CANVAS OR LEATHER STRIP, SOFT ENOUGH TO PUSH A NEEDLE THROUGH, AND FIRM ENOUGH TO PREVENT STRETCHING OUT OF SHAPE.

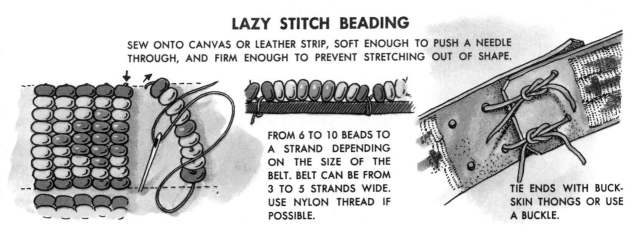

FROM 6 TO 10 BEADS TO A STRAND DEPENDING ON THE SIZE OF THE BELT. BELT CAN BE FROM 3 TO 5 STRANDS WIDE. USE NYLON THREAD IF POSSIBLE.

TIE ENDS WITH BUCKSKIN THONGS OR USE A BUCKLE.

BEADWORK (Continued)

Lazy stitch beading was used by the Plains Indians. While it looks better when done with selected beads, it will absorb odd size beads without giving your finished work a poor appearance. The Indians sewed on quite heavy buckskin or elk. They did not sew entirely through the material but just caught the outer surface of the hide. The best method for you, however, is to sew the beads entirely through the skin or cloth with waxed carpet thread. Beginners should not sew directly on the garment but should do their beadwork on heavy cloth, canvas, or felt. This in turn is sewed on to the garment.

Applique stitch beading is the type in which a thread of beads is appliqued or sewed on the cloth with a second needle and thread

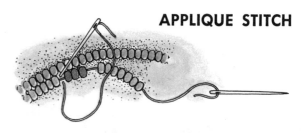

APPLIQUE STITCH

USING TWO NEEDLES AND TWO THREADS, SEW DOWN BETWEEN EVERY 2ND OR 3RD BEAD.

HOW TO MAKE ROSETTES

1. MAKE A 4½″ STRETCHER OF WILLOW OR ASH AND STRETCH A 3″ PIECE OF THIN LEATHER ON IT. USE HEAVY THREAD.

2. MARK AS SHOWN (SEE THUNDERBIRD DESIGN). ROSETTES ARE ABOUT 1⅞″ TO 2″ IN DIAMETER, OR 11 TO 12 ROWS OF BEADS.

3. KNOT NO. 60 THREAD AND SEW ON CENTER BEAD.

4. SEW DOWN FIRST ROW.

5. FROM NOW ON SEW DOWN FOUR AND GO BACK AND SEW DOWN THE LAST TWO AGAIN.

6. AFTER EACH ROW IS SEWED DOWN, RUN THE THREAD THROUGH THE ENTIRE ROW OF BEADS AGAIN TO EVEN THEM UP.

7. SEW LEATHER STRIP TO STIFF BACKING FOR LOOP. THEN MOUNT ROSETTE ON BACKING.

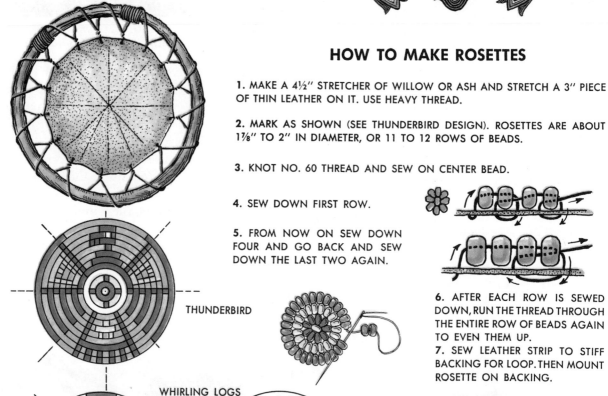

THUNDERBIRD

WHIRLING LOGS

¾ X 3¼″ LEATHER LOOP

STIFF BACKING

GLUE

FOLD OVER BACKING AND GLUE DOWN.

by catching the beading thread between every second or third bead. This method is used by both the Woodland and the Plains Indians for their floral design beadwork.

The applique design should be transferred onto cloth that is tacked to a frame to keep it flat. To applique small designs, such as rosettes, an embroidery hoop or willow stretcher can be used to hold the cloth or leather smooth and straight.

Imitation quill work, rather than real beadwork, is recommended for beginners and for articles that will get rough usage. When carefully done, it is very attractive. From a distance it cannot be detected from real quill work. Also it can be done in a lot less time than beadwork and is very inexpensive. The materials used are regular model airplane dope, several chisel-shaped sticks, a pocket knife, and an awl. If you make a mistake, it can be corrected by using airplane dope thinner. Scrape the old work off with a dull knife and start over. But work very, very carefully!

It is necessary to undercoat all design areas with a coat of clear lacquer (or fingernail polish) before the colored airplane dope is applied. This material is clear and can be applied directly over the outlines of the designs.

IMITATION QUILL WORK

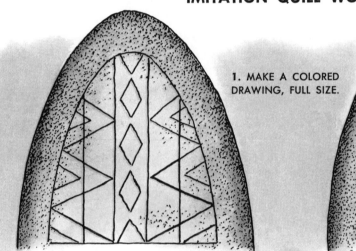

1. MAKE A COLORED DRAWING, FULL SIZE.

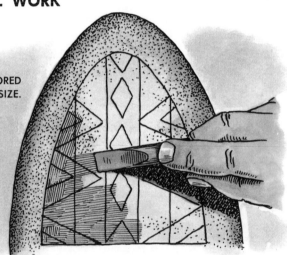

2. TRACE OR DRAW THE OUTLINES ON LEATHER WITH A SOFT PENCIL OR A BALL-POINT PEN.

3. GIVE AREA TO BE PAINTED A COAT OF CLEAR LACQUER AND SPREAD IT OUT SMOOTHLY WITH A CHISEL-EDGED STICK.

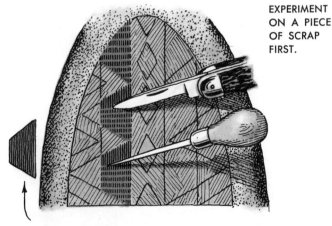

EXPERIMENT ON A PIECE OF SCRAP FIRST.

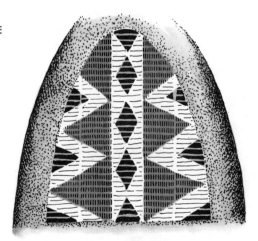

4. PAINT ONE COLOR AT A TIME. WHEN IT BEGINS TO SET, SCORE IT IN LINES 1/16" APART WITH A DULL KNIFE BLADE OR AN AWL, THROUGH TO THE LEATHER. USE AIRPLANE DOPE.

5. KEEP EACH SECTION SEPARATE. THIS SCORING WILL STAY "OPEN" AND WILL GIVE THE APPEARANCE OF QUILL WORK OR EVEN BEADWORK.

61

BEADWORK DESIGNS

BEADWORK beginners usually make the mistake of picking out designs that are much too elaborate and complicated for them to do. They soon become discouraged and a beading project that could be a lot of fun is given up as a failure.

Be smart. Start with a simple repeating design on a narrow hat band or belt not more than 10 or 11 inches long. If you make a mistake you can repair it without too much work. You can do a small piece of beadwork like this in a relatively short time. When you have finished, you will have a feeling of accomplishment and will look forward enthusiastically to doing your next piece.

To do good beadwork, you need a well made plan or design of what you are going to do. To make a plan, you need a set of colored pencils (not crayons because they are too large and soft). These colored pencils are hard and can be sharpened to a fairly sharp point. You will also need beadwork graph paper, something that is very difficult to obtain. Beadwork designs cannot be made on regular graph paper because the graphs are square and too big. The designs made on regular graph paper will be out of scale and cannot be reproduced accurately in beadwork. For this reason, we have inserted a blank page of beadwork graph paper on page 65. All you will have to do is get yourself a few sheets of tracing paper. Lay the tracing paper over the blank bead chart and hold it in place with cellophane tape. Then go ahead and fill in your design. You can make as many designs as you want in full color simply by changing to a new sheet of paper when necessary. Don't forget to use good taste in planning your design. Pick out design elements that are characteristic of the tribes you are studying and select colors that look well together.

In following authentic Indian beadwork it is allowable to modify design or change color. I think it should be remembered at all times that we are not trying to be real Indians. We are merely borrowing some of their arts and crafts for our own and others' enjoyment. Of course, you should not combine Woodland designs with Plains designs. The colors used for beading should be a matter of individual taste. Many authentic Indian beadwork designs are unpleasing to the white man, so do not use them. Many times the Indians used the beads that they had on hand. You will find yourself in exactly the same position and you must use your good judgment as to what to do.

White is usually a very good background color for all beadwork, especially if it is sewed on a dark base material. Turquoise backgrounds are very effective on buckskin or leather.

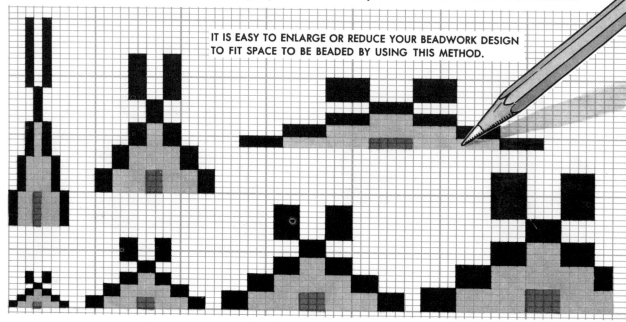

IT IS EASY TO ENLARGE OR REDUCE YOUR BEADWORK DESIGN TO FIT SPACE TO BE BEADED BY USING THIS METHOD.

63

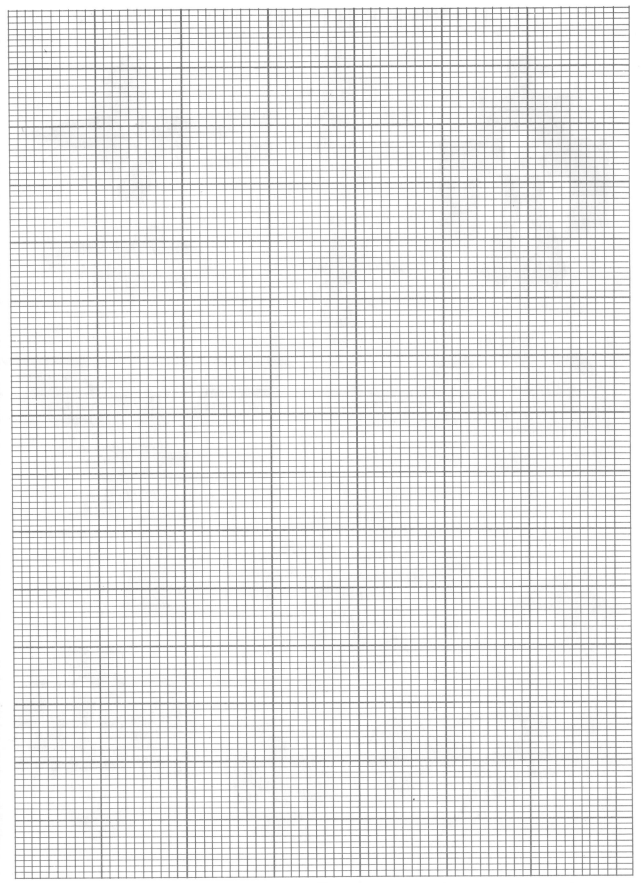

THUNDERBIRD DESIGNS

PUEBLO

ZIA

ZUNI KNIFE WING MAN
(OFTEN MISTAKEN FOR A BIRD)

OJIBWA

PIMA

ZIA RAIN BIRD

SOUTHWEST

ACOMA

THE mythical Thunderbird, in one form or another, was held in awe by practically all of the Indian tribes. On the Great Plains, where the phenomena of thunderstorms was very striking, the Thunderbird was supposed to be a deity in the form of a bird of enormous size, which produced thunder by flapping its wings, and lightning by opening and closing its eyes. These great birds were thought to carry a lake of fresh water on their backs, which caused a great downpour when they flew through the air.

Tribes of the Pacific Coast thought the Thunderbird caught whales during a thunderstorm and used its wings as a bow to shoot arrows. Each tribe interpreted the bird differently in its art, as shown on these two pages. The design of the Thunderbird was used to decorate war drums, pottery, and walls and was supposed to protect individuals and tribes from the Evil Spirits.

NORTHWEST COAST

MAGPIE

ARAPAHO EAGLE

SOUTHWEST

OTHER DESIGNS AND SYMBOLS

MANY other designs besides the Thunderbird were used by the Indians to decorate their clothing and pottery. Those shown here are from many sources and will be valuable in decorating your moccasins, vests, war drums, and tepees. Remember that the Indians used colors made from roots, berries, bark and fruits of plants and shrubs, as well as some mineral colors. These were very delicate colors, so keep that in mind when you use water colors and enamels.

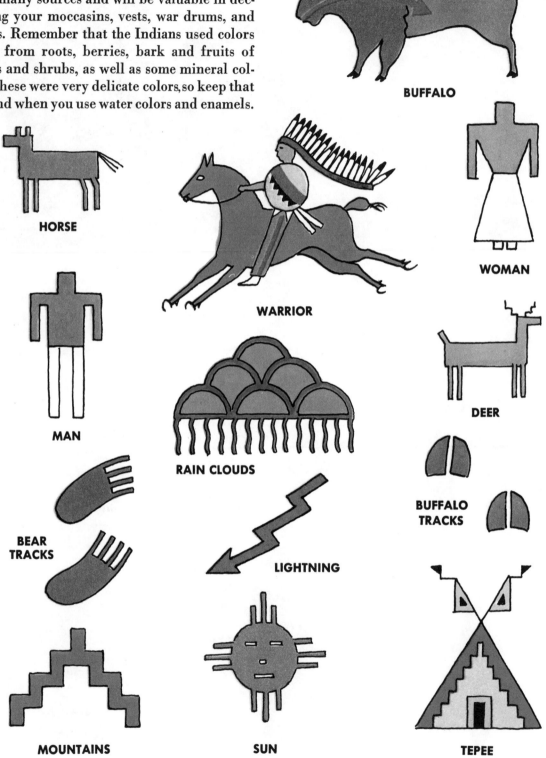

BUFFALO

HORSE

WARRIOR

WOMAN

MAN

RAIN CLOUDS

DEER

BEAR TRACKS

LIGHTNING

BUFFALO TRACKS

MOUNTAINS

SUN

TEPEE

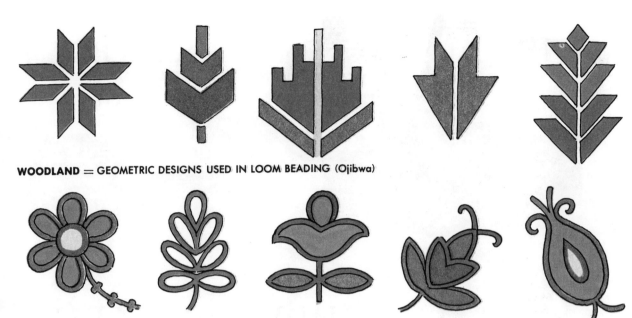

WOODLAND = GEOMETRIC DESIGNS USED IN LOOM BEADING (Ojibwa)

WOODLAND = FLORAL DESIGNS USED IN APPLIQUE BEADING (Ojibwa)

BLACKFOOT = GEOMETRIC AND FLORAL DESIGNS USUALLY APPLIQUED

SIOUX = GEOMETRIC BEADING, USUALLY DONE IN LAZY STITCH

UTE = GEOMETRIC **PUEBLO** = PAINTED DESIGNS

GREASE PAINTS

LEG Make-up DARK

SPONGE

CLEANSING TISSUE

—OR SOFT CLEAN CLOTHS

PANCAKE MAKE-UP

Cold Cream

INDIAN MAKE-UP

THE Indians painted their faces and bodies for several different reasons—sometimes for protection against the sun, wind, and insects. Some of the markings indicated memberships in various political or religious societies; others represented brave deeds done by the wearer. Many times the designs were merely personal decoration without any particular meaning.

The dry coloring matter was carried in small buckskin bags and was mixed with bear or buffalo fat before being rubbed on the skin. Clays containing oxide or iron were used for red; kaolin clay was used for white; black was made from wood charcoal; and green from

FIRST GO OVER LIDS AND WORK AROUND EYES.

BE SURE TO COVER THE EARS COMPLETELY.

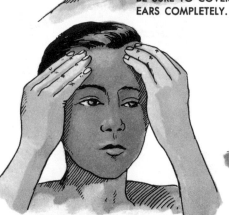

WORK MAKE-UP WELL INTO EDGE OF HAIRLINE. COVER FOREHEAD AND LOWER PART OF FACE.

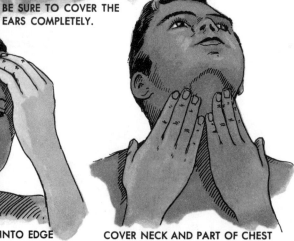

COVER NECK AND PART OF CHEST AND SHOULDERS THAT MAY SHOW. ALSO HANDS AND ARMS.

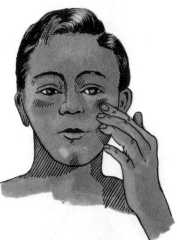

PUT A DAB OF ROUGE ON CHEEK BONES AND CHIN. BLEND EDGES.

powdered copper ore. Colors did not represent the same things in every tribe, but generally most tribes used black to represent death, red for human life, blue for sadness or trouble, white for peace or purity, and yellow for joy.

The best Indian make-up for a white person is a good deep tan. However, dark tan theatrical make-up or women's leg make-up may also be used. This make-up comes in liquid or cake form and can be applied with the fingers or a fine sponge. It is also easy to remove. Nothing spoils the effect more than a patch of paleface showing through, so be sure to apply make-up thoroughly.

Do not overpaint by putting too many symbols or markings on the face or body, since this will only detract from the effectiveness of your whole costume.

While the Indians frequently painted their entire body with a blue or white color, this is not recommended for Indian Lore ceremonials because the only colors available are theatrical paints mixed in oil, which are quite difficult to remove.

SUGGESTIONS FOR FACE MAKE-UP

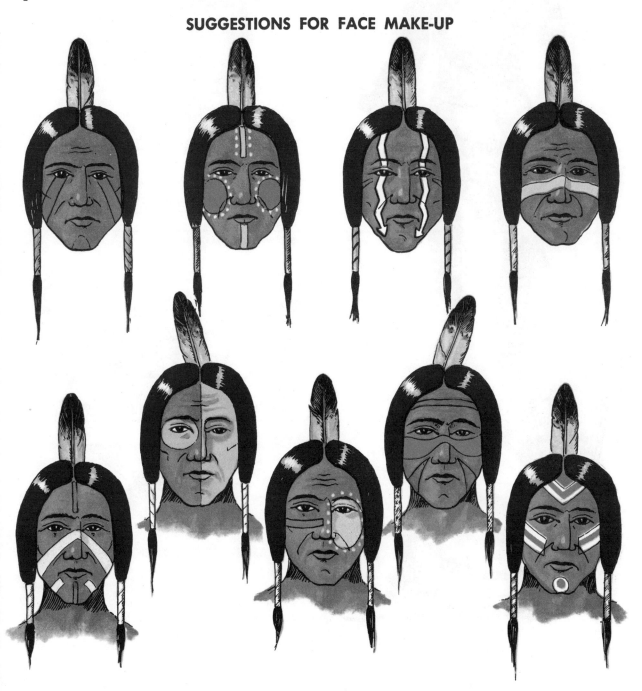

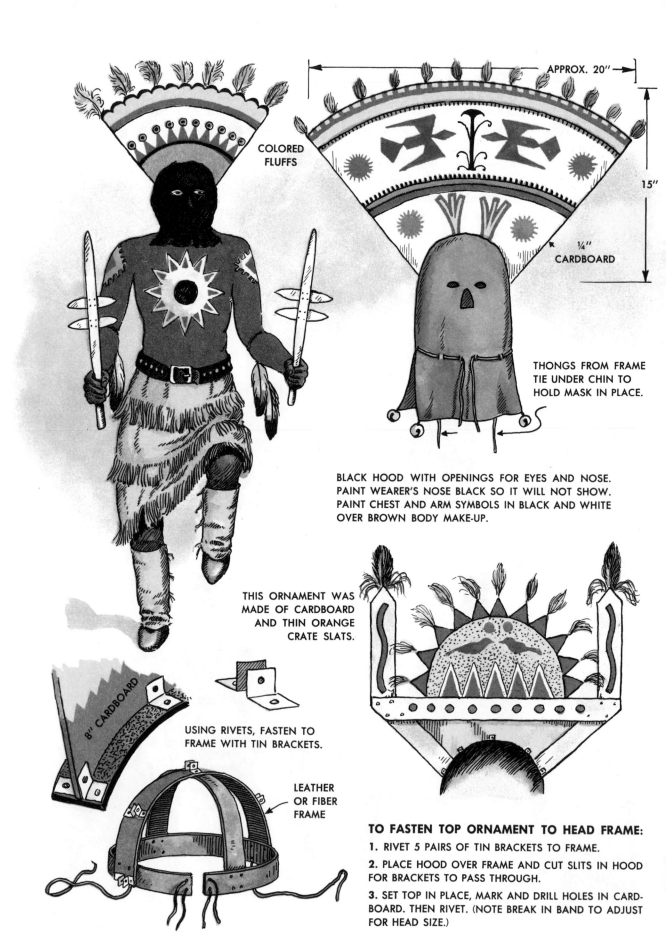

COLORED
FLUFFS

APPROX. 20"

15"

¼"
CARDBOARD

THONGS FROM FRAME
TIE UNDER CHIN TO
HOLD MASK IN PLACE.

BLACK HOOD WITH OPENINGS FOR EYES AND NOSE.
PAINT WEARER'S NOSE BLACK SO IT WILL NOT SHOW.
PAINT CHEST AND ARM SYMBOLS IN BLACK AND WHITE
OVER BROWN BODY MAKE-UP.

THIS ORNAMENT WAS
MADE OF CARDBOARD
AND THIN ORANGE
CRATE SLATS.

8" CARDBOARD

USING RIVETS, FASTEN TO
FRAME WITH TIN BRACKETS.

LEATHER
OR FIBER
FRAME

TO FASTEN TOP ORNAMENT TO HEAD FRAME:

1. RIVET 5 PAIRS OF TIN BRACKETS TO FRAME.

2. PLACE HOOD OVER FRAME AND CUT SLITS IN HOOD
FOR BRACKETS TO PASS THROUGH.

3. SET TOP IN PLACE, MARK AND DRILL HOLES IN CARD-
BOARD. THEN RIVET. (NOTE BREAK IN BAND TO ADJUST
FOR HEAD SIZE.)

72

THE DEVIL DANCE COSTUME

THE Apache Indians were wandering tribes who lived in the Southwest. Their dances are religious ceremonies in which they worship their gods: the sun, the moon, the planets, wind, rain, thunder, lightning, and certain animals. Many charms and fetishes are used in these ceremonies. The masks and headdresses are made under the supervision of a priest, and before they are assembled, the dancers go through the purifying ceremony of a sweat bath.

The medicine men's costumes of the Apache Devil Dance are very colorful and are all somewhat different. There are usually four dancers, one representing the devil.

Attached to the cloth mask which covers the face is a fan-shaped headdress made of thin narrow strips of yucca wood. These strips are arranged in many different ways and are painted with symbols representing the sun, moon, rain, stars, lightning, and so forth. Sometimes these designs were perforated through the thin slabs of wood. This fan is supposed to represent the spread tail feathers of a great bird. Sometimes turkey feathers were used on the headdress in place of the wooden fan.

The Apache medicine men made two sets of masks. These masks were used until it was felt that they had been worn out and had lost their magic powers. Then they were replaced with new masks, having strong and fresh medicine.

The costume shown here is a reproduction of those worn by the Apache crown dancers of the San Carlos reservation in New Mexico. It was drawn from photographs taken at the Gallup, New Mexico, Indian ceremonies.

LONG-SLEEVED UNDERSHIRT DYED BLACK WITH PAINTED WHITE DECO-RATIONS IN PLACE OF BODY PAINT.

BELLS

BELLS

SKIRT OF YELLOW BUCKSKIN OR DYED FLANNEL. CUT CLOTH FRINGE ½" WIDE WITH PINKING SHEARS, OR MAKE FRINGE OF SOFT LEATHER. THEN SEW ON SKIRT. ADD BELLS.

WANDS FROM 18 TO 24" LONG ARE MADE OF ¼" PINE AND PAINTED WHITE.

WEAR WIDE BLACK LEATHER BELT WITH BRASS STUDS AND SILVER CONCHAS.

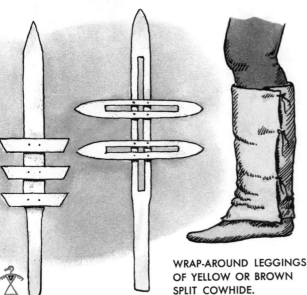

WRAP-AROUND LEGGINGS OF YELLOW OR BROWN SPLIT COWHIDE.

THE BUFFALO DANCE COSTUME

THE buffalo played a large part in the ceremonies and mythology of the Plains Indians. Many myths and folk tales about the buffalo, which delighted both young and old, were told and retold about the campfires.

The first buffalo spirit was supposed to have been born in a northern cave and was said to have been pure white. It had great powers in healing, especially wounds. A white buffalo in a herd was supposed to be the reappearance of this buffalo spirit on earth. The hide taken from such an animal was sacred and had special ceremonial purposes.

Most of the Plains tribes had buffalo societies. The members of these groups took part in special buffalo ceremonies and dances. These men had personal names suggesting movements, actions, or postures of the animal, such as "Standing Buffalo," or "Sitting Bull."

The Buffalo Dance of the Plains tribes has many forms. Sometimes a herd of buffalo are represented. In this dance we have only one buffalo wearing a buffalo mask and a buffalo tail. Other dancers, eight or more in number, are hunters carrying feathered lances and shields.

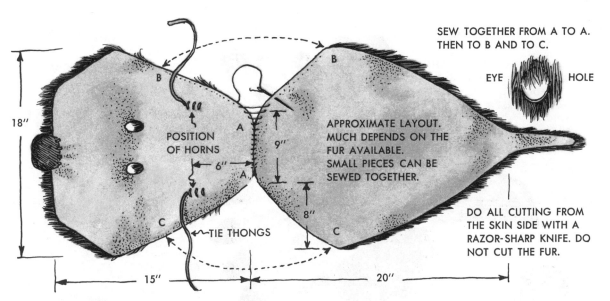

SEW TOGETHER FROM A TO A. THEN TO B AND TO C.

EYE HOLE

18"

B

B

POSITION OF HORNS

A

9"

APPROXIMATE LAYOUT. MUCH DEPENDS ON THE FUR AVAILABLE. SMALL PIECES CAN BE SEWED TOGETHER.

6"

A

8"

C

C

TIE THONGS

DO ALL CUTTING FROM THE SKIN SIDE WITH A RAZOR-SHARP KNIFE. DO NOT CUT THE FUR.

15"

20"

THIS MASK IS MADE OUT OF AN OLD BEARSKIN RUG. IT IS MADE OF TWO PIECES WITH THE HAIR RUNNING DOWNWARD. EYE OPENINGS ARE CUT OUT LAST. PUT ON THE MASK AND MARK WITH CHALK, ON THE INSIDE, THE POSITIONS FOR THE EYE OPENINGS. FUR IS ALWAYS SEWED TOGETHER FROM THE INSIDE, AS SHOWN.

8"

BLACK HORNS

CUT NOSE OF 2" WHITE PINE. PAINT NOSE BLACK AND NOSTRILS RED.

SAW CUT FOR FUR.

3½"

CUT HORNS OUT OF ¾" WHITE PINE AND ROUND THEM. THEN SEW TO FUR.

TAIL ABOUT 12 TO 14" LONG MADE OF BLACK LEATHER WITH TUFT OF HAIR TIED TO THE END. THIS BELT IS WORN OVER THE BREECH-CLOUT BELT.

PRAYER OVER DEAD BUFFALO

75

HEADPIECE

CROWN MAY BE COVERED WITH WHITE FLUFFS OR RABBIT FUR. FEATHERS MAY BE ADDED, BUT THEY MUST BE FASTENED ON FIRST.

START CEMENTING FLUFFS AT LOWER EDGE AND WORK UPWARD.

PAINT BEAK YELLOW.

EYES OF CARDBOARD TIED ON OVER FLUFFS.

BEAK

MAKE BEAK OF BALSA WITH ROUNDED TOP.

FASTEN WITH CEMENT AND THONGS.

BEAK MAY ALSO BE MADE OF FIBER AND GUMMED TAPE.

OLD FELT HAT CROWN

A WOODLAND ROACH CAN BE WORN IN PLACE OF THE EAGLE HEADPIECE.

TAIL

WOOD

FLUFFS

CEMENT AND TACK FEATHERS TO BLOCK AND COVER WITH FLUFFS.

WRAP-AROUND KILT

FASTEN WITH 2 LARGE SAFETY PINS

MAKE WRAP-AROUND KILT OF WHITE CANVAS. ADD SASH AS SHOWN ON NEXT PAGE AND DECORATE BOTH WITH BLACK AND RED PAINT.

SPATS

YELLOW YARN LEG BANDS OR BELLS MAY BE WORN.

BRIGHT YELLOW SPATS, WORN OVER MOCCASINS, ARE MADE OF SOFT PAINTED LEATHER. WRAP A PIECE OF CLOTH AROUND ANKLE TO GET YOUR PATTERN.

THE EAGLE DANCE COSTUME

USE BROWN BODY MAKE-UP WITH NO OTHER MARKINGS.

FROM 40 TO 60 FEATHERS ARE REQUIRED FOR THE WINGS. USE SMALL WHITE FEATHERS OR LARGE FLUFFS TO COVER UPPER PART.

NECK TIE THONGS

ARM TIE THONGS (2)

HAND POCKET

RED LINING CLOTH

CEMENT AND SEW

CEMENT

10"

WHITE CLOTH

WINGS

MOST Indian tribes considered the eagle a great and powerful spirit. His courage was admired, his strength envied. The great height to which this bird flew gave evidence that he could reach heaven, and his plumes were said to carry prayers.

The Eagle dance is one of the most graceful of all the Indian dances, and the costume is one of the most spectacular of all Southwestern dance costumes. The Eagles usually dance in pairs but there are a few solo dances.

There are several kinds of costumes. The one described here shows up equally well under bright lights or in the half light of a council fire. The length of the cloth part should be equal to the outstretched arms of an average boy, or about 5½ feet. Use 8- to 10-inch imitation eagle feathers. (See pp. 14-15.)

The costume portrayed here is a copy of one used by the Jemez (Hay'-mess) dancers. The Jemez pueblo is in northern New Mexico, about forty miles northwest of Albuquerque.

77

INDIAN LORE DANCING

RELIGIOUS DANCE

For basic Indian dance
steps, see pp. 80-81.

STORY DANCE

AFTER the costumes are made there are several things that can be done with them. They may be hung up for decorative purposes, or they may be used for pageants, rituals, and dancing. Of the three, dancing is the most popular, since a dance ceremonial is usually composed of groups of dancers trained and rehearsed individually.

A dance ceremonial can be organized easily if a sufficient number of dance groups can be assembled. Each group should perform from three to five minutes, depending upon the dance. Six or seven groups, each providing several dances, will make a good colorful hour or two of action-packed entertainment.

Most of the old Indian dances had very definite purposes. The Hopi Snake Dance and other dances of the Southwest were prayers for rain. Some dances were for healing purposes, some were for pleasure, some were for death, and some were for marriages.

In the old days the Indians danced the war dance to incite the warriors before they went into battle. When the braves returned, victory dances were held to celebrate their success.

Authentic Indian dances were never intended for general public entertainment. Many of the dances were very long and drawn out. For instance, the Sun Dance went on continuously day and night for several days until the dancers dropped from fatigue. This dance, by the way, is still practiced among certain tribes but has been modified considerably.

Indian lore dances are for entertainment only and should be planned as such. They should not be called authentic. Dances must be modified by taking the most spectacular parts out of the old dances. Program time is limited and your audience will quickly become bored if the dances are too slow and repetitive.

Each dance should be short, from three to ten minutes long. However, do not cut the dance so much that the audience cannot grasp the significance or spirit of it. Repeat fast action two or three times. A slow dance which is readily understood should be danced only once or twice. Remember that most audiences like a lot of color, action, and showmanship.

A narrator can do a lot to make or break a good Indian dance program. A public address system is a help, if it is not too loud or used too often. Remember, Indian dances are primitive and too much use of a loud speaker will spoil the effect. A short introduction before the dance explaining the dance, and a word or two during the dancing, will help the audience to appreciate your performance.

A SIMPLE DANCE WELL
DONE IS MUCH BETTER
THAN AN ELABORATE ONE
POORLY DONE.

SKILL DANCE

DEATH DANCE

VICTORY DANCE

THE CHIPPEWA SERPENTINE DANCE

AFTER first mastering the basic 1-2 and 1-2-3 steps (see pp. 80-81), try this dance. It is ideal for a beginners' class for it is very much like the familiar "Follow the Leader" game.

A good dancer should be the leader. He should start with the toe-heel step and change to various steps as the dance progresses. Any number of dancers may take part.

Like the old Grand March, the dance goes first around in a large circle, then across the stage, forming large figure eights as the dancers weave in and out. To make the dance effective, the dancers should be evenly spaced, changing steps only at a loud drum signal.

This is a fun dance. The trick is to change steps immediately at the change in the drum beat. The tempo is varied from slow to fast.

The dance is very spectacular when danced in perfect unison, ending with the dancers turning in the last steps to face the audience.

79

BASIC INDIAN DANCE STEPS

THE 1-2 or Toe-Heel Step is one of the simplest and yet one of the most generally used of all Indian dance steps. A beginner can learn the step positions in a few minutes, but it will require considerable practice to develop the proper rhythm and enough coordination of the steps to dance with other dancers.

The best way to teach this step is to line up a group of six to twelve beginners and have them do the step positions in unison without moving from the spot on which they are standing.

The loud and soft beat of the drum must be clearly heard by all of the dancers, because each of the steps is timed to these beats.

There are two dance positions. The first is made on the loud No. 1 beat of the drum. On this beat step up with the left foot and touch the ground lightly with the toe. The second position is made on the soft No. 2 beat of the drum by coming down hard on the heel. Alternate by doing these two positions, first on the left foot, then on the right. The drummer should start and stop over and over until the entire group can start and stop in unison. When everyone has caught on to the step, the dancers can start to dance slowly forward in a circle. Then try some of the other variations of this step such as dancing backwards or from side to side.

THE 1-2 OR TOE-HEEL STEP

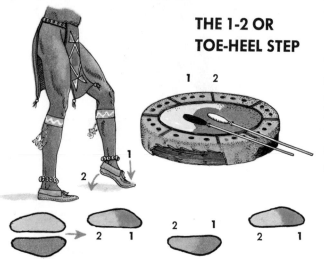

THE STOMP STEP

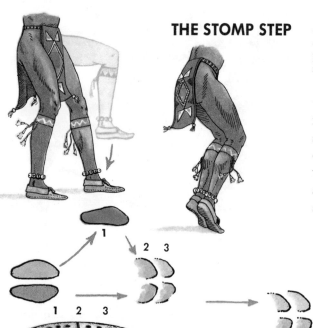

The Stomp Step is much more emphatic than the toe-heel dance step. The dancer's body is held upright and the hands are kept close to the body at hip height. The dance is timed to the 1-2-3 drum beat and has three dance positions. On the 1 beat, the knee is lifted high and the foot brought down hard to the ground in a stomping motion. On the 2-3 light beat the dancer comes down lightly in two hops on the toes. Most of the action is done with the hands and arms. The drum rhythm must be evenly spaced to a 1-2-3, and not 1—2-3 beat.

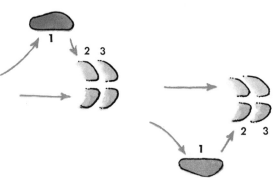

80

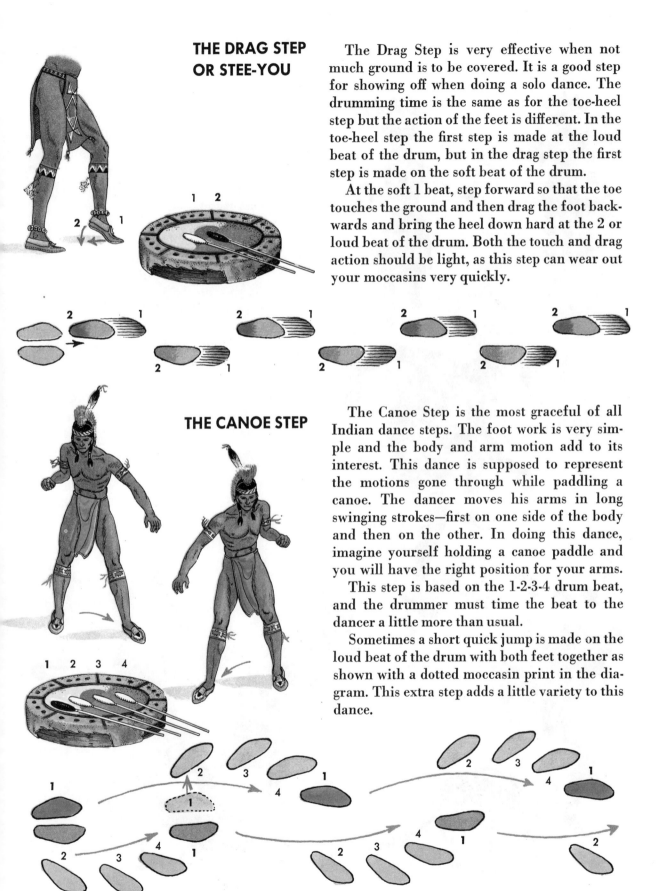

THE DRAG STEP OR STEE-YOU

The Drag Step is very effective when not much ground is to be covered. It is a good step for showing off when doing a solo dance. The drumming time is the same as for the toe-heel step but the action of the feet is different. In the toe-heel step the first step is made at the loud beat of the drum, but in the drag step the first step is made on the soft beat of the drum.

At the soft 1 beat, step forward so that the toe touches the ground and then drag the foot backwards and bring the heel down hard at the 2 or loud beat of the drum. Both the touch and drag action should be light, as this step can wear out your moccasins very quickly.

THE CANOE STEP

The Canoe Step is the most graceful of all Indian dance steps. The foot work is very simple and the body and arm motion add to its interest. This dance is supposed to represent the motions gone through while paddling a canoe. The dancer moves his arms in long swinging strokes—first on one side of the body and then on the other. In doing this dance, imagine yourself holding a canoe paddle and you will have the right position for your arms.

This step is based on the 1-2-3-4 drum beat, and the drummer must time the beat to the dancer a little more than usual.

Sometimes a short quick jump is made on the loud beat of the drum with both feet together as shown with a dotted moccasin print in the diagram. This extra step adds a little variety to this dance.

THE APACHE DEVIL DANCE

THE costumes shown here are for the Apache medicine men who are the good spirits in this colorful dance. The Devil is usually dressed in a breechclout with a black hood over his head.

The dance varies greatly in detail, but the general theme is always the same: the conflict between the evil and good spirits, climaxed by the success of the good.

The dance begins as a warrior comes out into the dance area and dances about in a happy, light-hearted manner. He hasn't a care in the world. Suddenly the Devil appears out of the darkness and slowly approaches the warrior, circling around him and making menacing passes at him with his hands. The warrior cannot see the Devil, but he begins to feel his evil influence. Gradually he becomes bewildered and weakened as the Devil becomes bolder and circles closer. Finally he slowly sinks to the ground. The Devil then rejoices and dances around the fallen warrior.

A medicine man then appears, views the fallen warrior, and in grotesque, stomping steps dances toward the Devil. The Devil is not afraid and defies the medicine man. When the medicine man sees he can do nothing alone, he retires to the rear of the stage.

MEDICINE MEN DANCE IN STIFF 1-2 STEPS

THE HAPPY WARRIOR DANCES JOYOUSLY

THE DEVIL WAVES THE HORSE HAIR WANDS LIKE CLAW-ING FINGERS

THE WARRIOR FALLS UNDER THE EVIL POWER OF THE DEVIL

THE POWER OF THE MEDICINE MAN IS TOO WEAK TO DRIVE OFF THE EVIL ONE

THE DEVIL REJOICES OVER THE FALLEN WARRIOR

Two or three more medicine men now appear, usually dressed in a costume similar to that of the first medicine man or sometimes with only the masks and the wands. The battle between the good spirits and the bad spirit then takes place.

The Devil at first is bold and defies them, but gradually the good spirits overcome him. Usually the Devil sinks away and the medicine men revive the fallen warrior and they dance happily off together.

The medicine men dance a stiff type of step, with knees bent and feet apart. Their postures are rather grotesque.

I have seen this dance performed with one warrior, one Devil, and one medicine man. The dancing or rather the gesturing of the Devil was a show in itself and was very fascinating. The Devil was dressed entirely in black and held a large wand of horse hair in each hand which gave the effect of long black fingers. He circled around the warrior slowly and held him in his spell until the medicine men drove him off. The theme was always the same—the good spirits gradually predominating over the evil spirit.

The dance is best performed at night under subdued lights or by a single camp fire, with the dancers appearing mysteriously out of the dark and disappearing the same way.

THE WARRIOR IS REVIVED BY THE GOOD SPIRITS

THE MEDICINE MEN RETURN WITH POWERFUL MEDICINE

THE EVIL SPIRIT IS DEFEATED

IF YOU ARE EVER IN THE VICINITY OF THE SAN CARLOS RESERVATION NEAR GALLUP, NEW MEXICO, BE SURE TO SEE THE INDIAN DANCE CEREMONIALS.

For basic Indian dance steps, see pp. 80-81.

83

BEND WOOD AROUND SOME OBJECT, SUCH AS A BARREL.

WOODEN HOOP

REGARDLESS OF THE KIND OF WOOD YOU USE, CUT A LONG SPLICE, FASTEN IT WITH 2 OR 3 CLINCHED NAILS, AND WRAP SPLICE WITH CORD AND CEMENT, OR WITH FRICTION TAPE. THIS FORMS GRIP.

PAINT HOOPS WHITE OR YELLOW AND DECORATE WITH COLORED FLUFFS OR RIBBON.

ALUMINUM HOOP

CAN BE USED IN PLACE OF WOODEN HOOP OR FOR THE FLAMING HOOP DANCE.

WOODEN PLUG

2" STRIP OF WIRE SCREENING

TAPE

BURLAP

FIGURE 1

FIGURE 2

THE HOOP DANCE

THE Indian Hoop Dance is one of the most spectacular of all the North American Indian dances.

The hoop is usually a solo dance, one which requires a lot of practice by even an experienced dancer. It originated among the Southwest tribes but is now used by dancers wherever Indian ceremonies are performed.

The Indians usually make dance hoops of some tough straight-grain wood. This wood may be split out of a section of a log. But more often a thin sapling of maple, ash, elm, or birch trimmed down to a uniform thickness of ½ to ⅝ inch is used. The best wood of all is ½-inch rattan, such as is used for making porch furniture. This wood is imported and must be purchased from dealers in porch furniture or basketry materials.

The hoop size for an experienced dancer is 20 inches. For a beginner it should be 22 to 24 inches in diameter. These hoops must be pliable and tough enough to be stood upon or bent without being broken.

84

Study the pictures carefully to see how the hoops are handled. In Figures 1 and 2, the hoop is swung upward over the upraised foot and passed over the opposite arm, head, and shoulders and then down over the body, as shown, and off the opposite foot. Every hoop dancer uses and perfects many plays. Usually he manipulates the hoop with the left and right hands alternately. It must be emphasized that every action is timed to the 1-2 beat, regardless of how intricately one manipulates the hoop or hoops.

The hoop can be thrown down, picked up by slipping the toes under it, and gradually wiggled up over the hips without the use of the hands. (Figure 3.)

The dancer may "walk the hoop." (Figure 4.) He may throw the hoop up and catch it on his upper arms. Whatever tricks he does must be done quickly to mystify the audience.

A fast hoop dancer goes from one manipulation to the next in rapid succession. Some dancers may, after doing each trick, walk a few steps, usually for applause, before doing the next one. Some dancers do a very rapid rope-jumping act for the grand finale by jumping forward through the hoop several times and then backward several times.

The hoop dance requires a lot of practice regardless of what way it is done. It is judged by the smoothness of the action. It is better to do a good job with one or two hoops than to fumble with too many.

For the flaming hoop dance, ⅜ or ½ inch aluminum tubing makes a very fine practical hoop. Fasten the ends together with a wooden dowel. Then counter-sink two flat-headed screws through the aluminum into the wooden plug. The section of the hoop that will be burning should be wrapped with burlap and then with wire screening to keep pieces of burning burlap from falling off. For the flaming hoop dance, the hoop should be at least 24 inches in diameter. A 2-foot section should be wrapped with friction tape for handling.

The flaming hoop dance is very spectacular at night but should not be attempted by an amateur. The dancer's hair should be well wetted down to prevent his hair from catching fire.

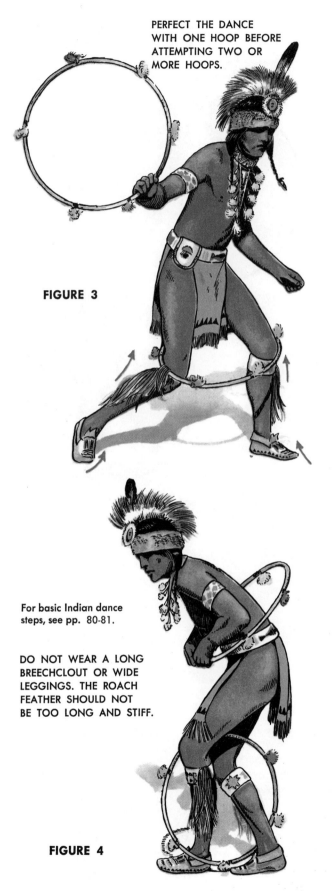

PERFECT THE DANCE WITH ONE HOOP BEFORE ATTEMPTING TWO OR MORE HOOPS.

FIGURE 3

For basic Indian dance steps, see pp. 80-81.

DO NOT WEAR A LONG BREECHCLOUT OR WIDE LEGGINGS. THE ROACH FEATHER SHOULD NOT BE TOO LONG AND STIFF.

FIGURE 4

THE BUFFALO DANCE

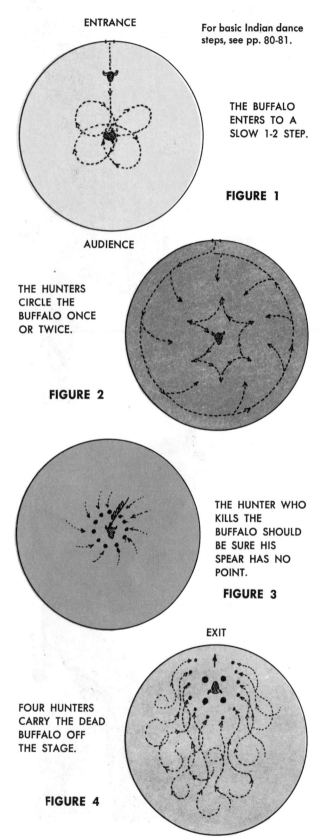

ENTRANCE

For basic Indian dance steps, see pp. 80-81.

THE BUFFALO ENTERS TO A SLOW 1-2 STEP.

FIGURE 1

AUDIENCE

THE HUNTERS CIRCLE THE BUFFALO ONCE OR TWICE.

FIGURE 2

THE HUNTER WHO KILLS THE BUFFALO SHOULD BE SURE HIS SPEAR HAS NO POINT.

FIGURE 3

EXIT

FOUR HUNTERS CARRY THE DEAD BUFFALO OFF THE STAGE.

FIGURE 4

THE buffalo enters first to a fairly slow 1-2 step, wandering aimlessly until he reaches the center of the dance area, grazing around and turning his head from side to side. (Figure 1.) Then the hunters enter, carrying spears and shields and dancing clockwise to a faster 1-2 step so that their shields, held on the left arm, are in full view of the audience.

At a signal the dancers discover and turn toward the buffalo. They stop for a second or two, then dance toward him to a little faster 1-2 tempo. The buffalo sees them and becomes very angry. He tosses his head and stamps his feet, all to the same 1-2 rhythm, swinging from side to side and charging the hunters, in short angry spurts. The hunters thrust their spears at him and dance back out of his way. Finally, one hunter, bolder than the rest, thrusts his spear into the side of the buffalo.

The spear is thrust between the buffalo's arm and body from the rear and is held in position by the buffalo, who then staggers about and finally drops face down with the spear sticking straight up into the air.

The hunters dance back and watch him die, keeping time with the 1-2 step. The hunters then dance a slower 1-2 step toward the fallen buffalo, gradually converging until they form a tight ring around him. At a signal, they all drop to one knee, their spears held upright and the butts brought down in unison with a single thud. The drum beat is very soft. The hunters then bow their heads in a silent prayer, thanking the great Wah Kanda (Great Spirit) for their good fortune and asking the buffalo's forgiveness. (Figure 3.) This quiet action is very impressive and should last only a few seconds.

At a signal, all of the hunters leap up and dance around madly while the dead buffalo is carried off the stage. (Figure 4.)

The happy dancing hunters should form a tight group around the dead buffalo as he is being removed, hiding him from the audience because he will probably be too heavy for four boys to lift and they will be dragging him. If lights are used, they should then be turned out.

THE EAGLE DANCE

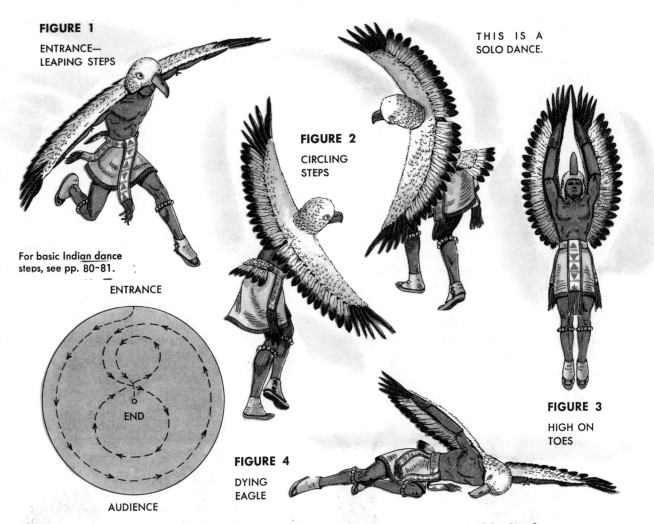

FIGURE 1

ENTRANCE—
LEAPING STEPS

For basic Indian dance
steps, see pp. 80-81.

ENTRANCE

END

AUDIENCE

FIGURE 2

CIRCLING
STEPS

THIS IS A
SOLO DANCE.

FIGURE 3

HIGH ON
TOES

FIGURE 4

DYING
EAGLE

IN this dance, as in any other good dance, the drummer plays an important part. He must watch every step. Without perfect synchronization between the drummer and the dancer, this dance is a failure.

The eagle enters slowly and gracefully soars around, dipping his wings slowly and progressing forward in long leaping steps to a 1-2 beat. As a rule one large circle is sufficient. If the stage is very small, he may circle twice. Then the eagle makes a figure eight, banking gracefully and at intervals giving a high "Ku-e-e Kee-e-e" call. The figure eight can be repeated. The eagle then comes slowly to the center of the stage facing the audience, gradually raising his wings as he comes to a dead stop. His wings come up slowly, quivering until the tips touch above him. The dancer is up on his toes. As this

is a difficult pose to hold, the drummer must also be "on his toes." At the very moment the eagle stretches to his fullest height, the drummer "shoots." The shot is one loud beat on the drum. The eagle screams "Ku-e-e Kee-e-e" and flutters about wildly in a circle. At the same time he gradually sinks lower and lower beating one wing, and holding the other limp. He falls, holding one wing up. When prone, he keeps beating with the one good wing against his body. Gradually this beating becomes less and less, and finally the wing falls limply. The drumming becomes softer and softer, dying out with the death of the bird.

If lights are used, it is very effective to lower them gradually in keeping with the drum, until they go out with the death of the bird. Keep the stage dark while the eagle retires from the stage.

87

INDIAN DANCE DRUMMING

GOOD drumming is very important in Indian dancing. Far too little emphasis has been placed on it. The rhythm must be carried by the drummer, who is the orchestra and the conductor at the same time. As in all stage dancing, the timing must be synchronized with the dancer. The drummer always must watch the feet of the dancers and beat out a steady, even rhythm. If you observe a really good Indian drummer, you will see that he keeps his eyes on the feet of the performers at all times. He never lets them rove around the room to watch the audience.

If there are two or more drummers, it is most important that they beat in unison. In order to accomplish this, one must act as the leader, while the other drummers follow his beat. There is nothing more disturbing to both the audience and the dancers than drummers who are not beating in unison. In many dances the drummer frequently must give a signal for a change in time and steps.

Many times I have sat and watched the Chippewa dance ceremonies and have taken particular notice of the drummers. Four old men sit around a large dance drum. They are all in perfect time with their leader. They start and stop all on the same beat.

Dance drumming should be timed to the slower dancer rather than to the fast one. A fast dancer can always dance slower, but it is extremely difficult for a slow dancer to dance fast. If the dance is to be a fast one, the director or leader should weed out the slow dancers. They can stand on the side lines and keep time to the drums, while the faster dancers in the center of the dance area execute the dance. In this way the slower and inexperienced dancers will not be totally eliminated, nor will the effectiveness of the dance suffer because of them.

Everyone who is interested in drumming for Indian dancing should read Bernard Mason's book called *Drums, Tom-toms, and Rattles.*

SOUTHWESTERN DRUMMER

CHIPPEWA DRUMMERS

BLACKFOOT DRUMMER

88

DRUMS AND TOM-TOMS

Music plays a very important part in the life of the American Indian. From the time he is born until he dies, his life is marked by dancing, and the drum is the keynote of it all.

There are three major types of drums—the small hand drum, usually with one head, commonly called the tom-tom and shown here. Other types (not shown) are the larger two-headed drum made from a hollowed-out log or keg, and the water drum, with a single removable head.

The drum heads are usually of rawhide, made from calf or deerskin. The drums are usually decorated with painted symbols and designs having religious or protective meanings. The American Indian never plays the drum by tapping it with his fist or hand—this is an African method. A drumstick is always used.

SINGLE HEAD TOM-TOM

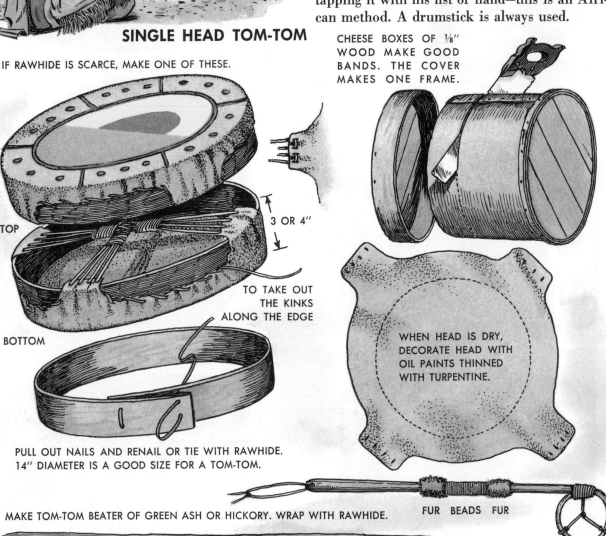

IF RAWHIDE IS SCARCE, MAKE ONE OF THESE.

TOP

BOTTOM

3 OR 4"

TO TAKE OUT
THE KINKS
ALONG THE EDGE

CHEESE BOXES OF ⅛"
WOOD MAKE GOOD
BANDS. THE COVER
MAKES ONE FRAME.

WHEN HEAD IS DRY,
DECORATE HEAD WITH
OIL PAINTS THINNED
WITH TURPENTINE.

PULL OUT NAILS AND RENAIL OR TIE WITH RAWHIDE.
14" DIAMETER IS A GOOD SIZE FOR A TOM-TOM.

MAKE TOM-TOM BEATER OF GREEN ASH OR HICKORY. WRAP WITH RAWHIDE.

FUR BEADS FUR

89

CUT OUT BOTTOM OF TUB OR BARREL WITH
KEYHOLE SAW, AS SHOWN, LEAVING ABOUT
3" STAND. NAIL ALL AROUND TO PREVENT
RATTLING.

CUT A NEW BOTTOM OF ⅜"
PLYWOOD. DRIVE IT DOWN AND
NAIL IT IN PLACE BEFORE CUT-
TING OFF BOTTOM SECTION.

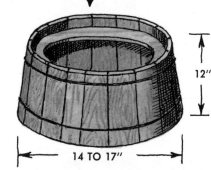

CUT RAWHIDE TO SHAPE
BEFORE SOAKING IT.
THEN STRETCH AS YOU
TACK IT TO TOP AND
BOTTOM.

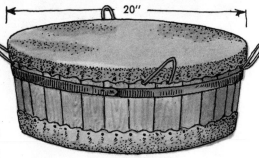

ORDER OF THE ARROW DRUMHEAD

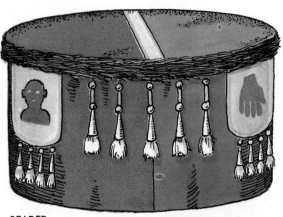

BEADED
TABS

ANOTHER TYPE OF SKIRT

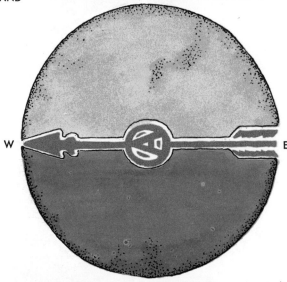

W   E

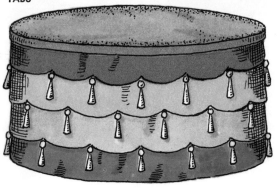

TO CONSERVE ON STOR-
AGE SPACE, YOU CAN
MAKE A DREAM DRUM
LIKE THIS. LONG SKIRT
CAMOUFLAGES THIN
DRUM.

CHIPPEWA DANCE DRUM

THE Chippewa Dream Dance ceremony is an outdoor dance, held early in July, around a large, elaborately decorated drum called the Dream Drum. The Dream Drum is very sacred and is supposed to possess strong spirits.

The drum is hung by hardwood hooks to four posts. On the tip of each post hangs an eagle feather prepared the same way as feathers for a headdress (pp. 14-15). Dream Drum heads should have a stripe, several inches wide, running across the head directly through the middle. When the Dream Drum is used for a dance ceremony, the drum should be placed so that this stripe runs from east to west. This line represents the path of the sun as it goes across the heavens from east to west.

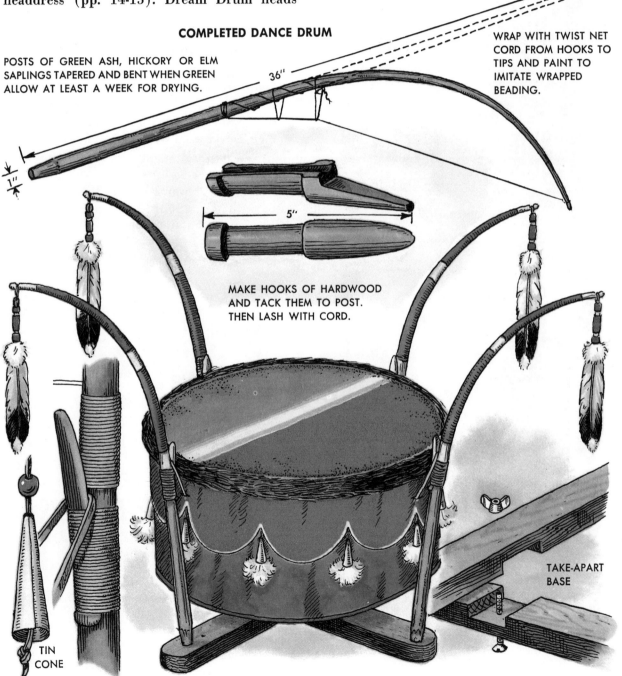

COMPLETED DANCE DRUM

POSTS OF GREEN ASH, HICKORY OR ELM SAPLINGS TAPERED AND BENT WHEN GREEN ALLOW AT LEAST A WEEK FOR DRYING.

36"

1"

WRAP WITH TWIST NET CORD FROM HOOKS TO TIPS AND PAINT TO IMITATE WRAPPED BEADING.

5"

MAKE HOOKS OF HARDWOOD AND TACK THEM TO POST. THEN LASH WITH CORD.

TAKE-APART BASE

TIN CONE

91

GIRL'S WOODLAND COSTUME

The women of the Woodland tribes wore dresses made of soft deerskin. When Army and trade blankets were introduced in the Indian territory, the women started to use them for their dresses.

The costumes shown on these pages are the two-piece style, although the Woodland women sometimes made a one-piece dress similar to the Plains costumes.

Indian women did not wear full-length leggings. Their leggings came to just beneath the knee, fastened with tie thongs or a garter.

The Woodland Indian woman usually wore her hair in braids with a bit of ribbon tied to the ends. In later years beaded bands were worn.

Woodland Indian women, like the Plains women, never used war paint. They sometimes applied a spot of rouge to the cheeks and chin.

Moccasins worn by women and girls were very much of the same style as the men's, decorated with bead or quill work in traditional tribal designs and patterns.

In the winter time both the Plains and the Woodland women wore blankets for warmth.

LEGGINGS

JEWELRY

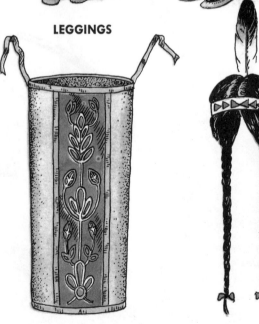

7
BEADS

15
BEADS

WOMEN'S LEGGINGS ADD MUCH TO THE COSTUME AND PROTECT THE ANKLES FROM INSECT BITES. USE RIBBON AND BEADWORK FOR DECORATION. FASTEN LEGGINGS BELOW KNEES.

A BLACK WIG IS A MUST UNLESS HAIR IS NATURALLY BLACK. USE A BEADED BROWBAND WITH 1 OR 2 FEATHERS FASTENED TO IT.

LOOM
BEADED

SMALL
COWRIE
SHELLS

NARROW BUCKSKIN THONGS, LEATHER SEPARATIONS, ROUND NECK BEADS, AND TUBULAR BEADS.

92

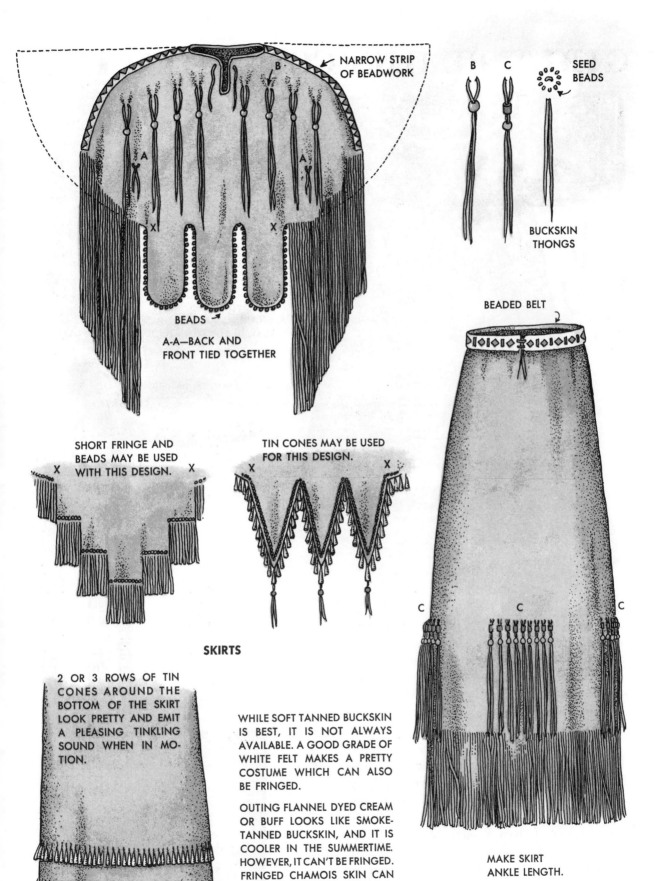

NARROW STRIP
OF BEADWORK

B

SEED
BEADS

BUCKSKIN
THONGS

BEADS →

A-A—BACK AND
FRONT TIED TOGETHER

SHORT FRINGE AND
BEADS MAY BE USED
WITH THIS DESIGN.

TIN CONES MAY BE USED
FOR THIS DESIGN.

BEADED BELT

SKIRTS

2 OR 3 ROWS OF TIN
CONES AROUND THE
BOTTOM OF THE SKIRT
LOOK PRETTY AND EMIT
A PLEASING TINKLING
SOUND WHEN IN MO-
TION.

WHILE SOFT TANNED BUCKSKIN
IS BEST, IT IS NOT ALWAYS
AVAILABLE. A GOOD GRADE OF
WHITE FELT MAKES A PRETTY
COSTUME WHICH CAN ALSO
BE FRINGED.

OUTING FLANNEL DYED CREAM
OR BUFF LOOKS LIKE SMOKE-
TANNED BUCKSKIN, AND IT IS
COOLER IN THE SUMMERTIME.
HOWEVER, IT CAN'T BE FRINGED.
FRINGED CHAMOIS SKIN CAN
BE SEWED ON, OR TIN CONES
MAY BE USED.

MAKE SKIRT
ANKLE LENGTH.

GIRL'S PLAINS COSTUME

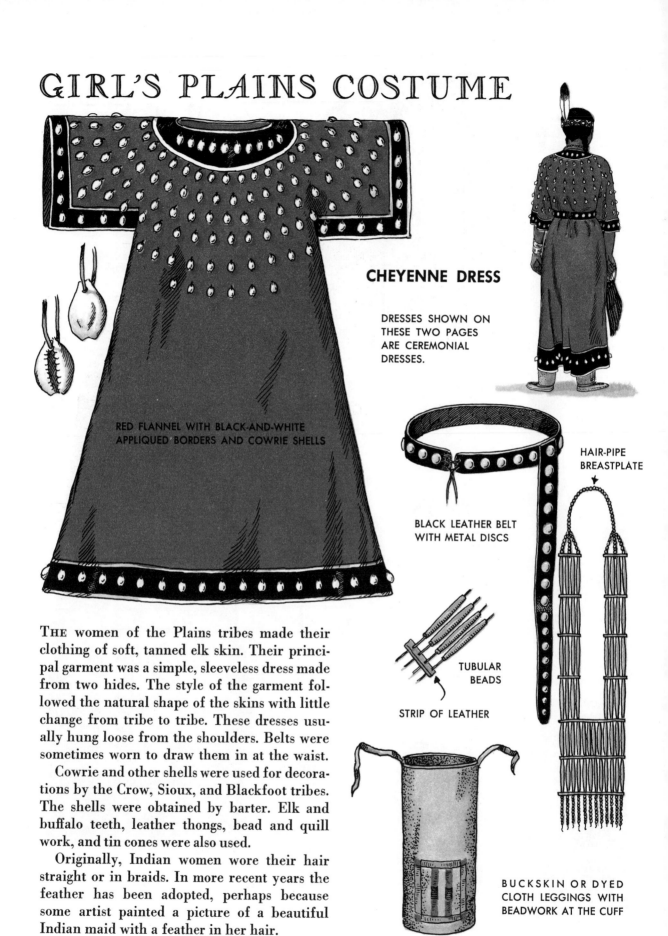

CHEYENNE DRESS

DRESSES SHOWN ON THESE TWO PAGES ARE CEREMONIAL DRESSES.

RED FLANNEL WITH BLACK-AND-WHITE APPLIQUED BORDERS AND COWRIE SHELLS

BLACK LEATHER BELT WITH METAL DISCS

HAIR-PIPE BREASTPLATE

TUBULAR BEADS

STRIP OF LEATHER

BUCKSKIN OR DYED CLOTH LEGGINGS WITH BEADWORK AT THE CUFF

THE women of the Plains tribes made their clothing of soft, tanned elk skin. Their principal garment was a simple, sleeveless dress made from two hides. The style of the garment followed the natural shape of the skins with little change from tribe to tribe. These dresses usually hung loose from the shoulders. Belts were sometimes worn to draw them in at the waist.

Cowrie and other shells were used for decorations by the Crow, Sioux, and Blackfoot tribes. The shells were obtained by barter. Elk and buffalo teeth, leather thongs, bead and quill work, and tin cones were also used.

Originally, Indian women wore their hair straight or in braids. In more recent years the feather has been adopted, perhaps because some artist painted a picture of a beautiful Indian maid with a feather in her hair.

BLACKFOOT DRESS

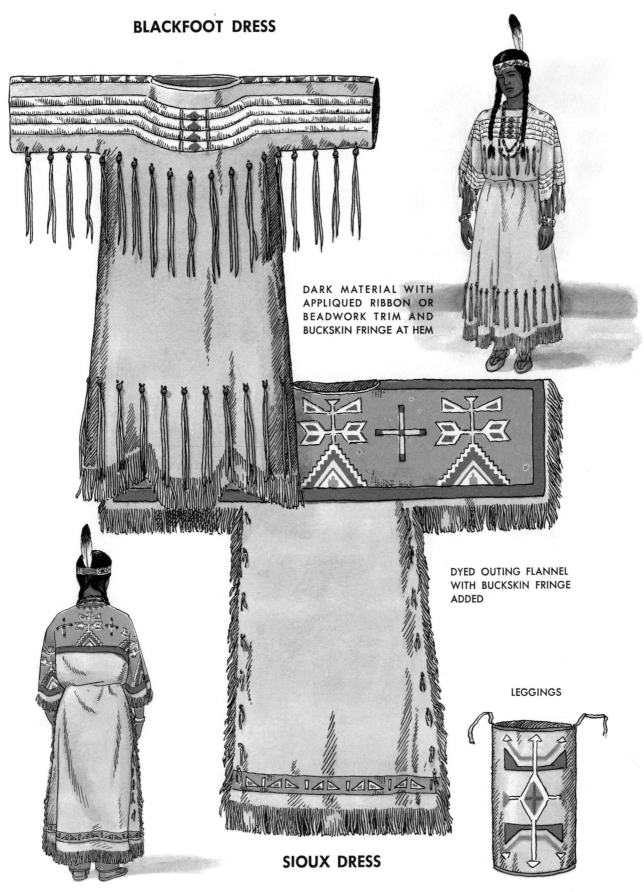

DARK MATERIAL WITH
APPLIQUED RIBBON OR
BEADWORK TRIM AND
BUCKSKIN FRINGE AT HEM

DYED OUTING FLANNEL
WITH BUCKSKIN FRINGE
ADDED

LEGGINGS

SIOUX DRESS

INDIAN TEPEE

THE typical dwelling of the Plains tribes is the tepee, or tipi. Tepee is a Sioux word: TI (dwelling) and PI (used for).

The tepee is considered the most perfect tent and has been copied in many forms. Originally the Indians made their tepees of buffalo hides, but since the destruction of the buffalo herds by the white man, domestic cow hides have been used, as well as canvas. New buffalo-hide tepee covers were made every spring. The size of the tepee depended somewhat on the number of horses the tribe or family had, because it required several horses to transport a large tepee. The poles were made of lodgepole pine, cedar, spruce, or any other straight tree. Flexible poles were not used. The poles averaged about 25 feet in length and tapered from 4 to 1 inch in diameter.

In warm weather the lower part of the tepee was raised up on the poles to allow the breeze to blow through. In cold weather the space around the bottom between the stakes and the ground was packed with sod to hold it down tightly and to keep out the snow and drafts.

When the tepee was new it was nearly white. But by spring, the smoke and the weather had darkened it at the top and the skins became quite transparent. At night the campfires made the tepees look like large Japanese lanterns.

On the Great Plains the wind is usually from the west and for that reason the tepees were set up with the smoke hole facing the east. The flaps, or smoke hole ears, as they are called, were used to control the drafts and to keep the wind from blowing down the smoke hole. In case of a storm they could be lapped over to close the smoke hole completely.

Some of the large 18- and 20-foot Blackfoot tepees are made of unbleached muslin. A good serviceable tepee can be made of this material or of drill. These materials are easily sewed together on any sewing machine and make a lighter tepee than canvas. The tepee shown on pp. 98-99 is made of 30-inch drill. To start, sew the 9-foot 4-inch piece to the long 28-foot 10-inch piece. Lay out according to the drawing and do all of the required work on these two pieces before sewing on the remaining pieces.

PINS OF ⅜″ BIRCH DOWELS 12″ LONG. TAPER THE ENDS.

TRIPOD LASHING

COMPLETED TEPEE SET UP. NOTE HOW SMOKE FLAPS ARE TIED AT BOTTOM. SMOKE FLAP POLES ARE CROSSED IN BACK. FLAPS ARE ADJUSTED ACCORDING TO DIRECTION OF WIND.

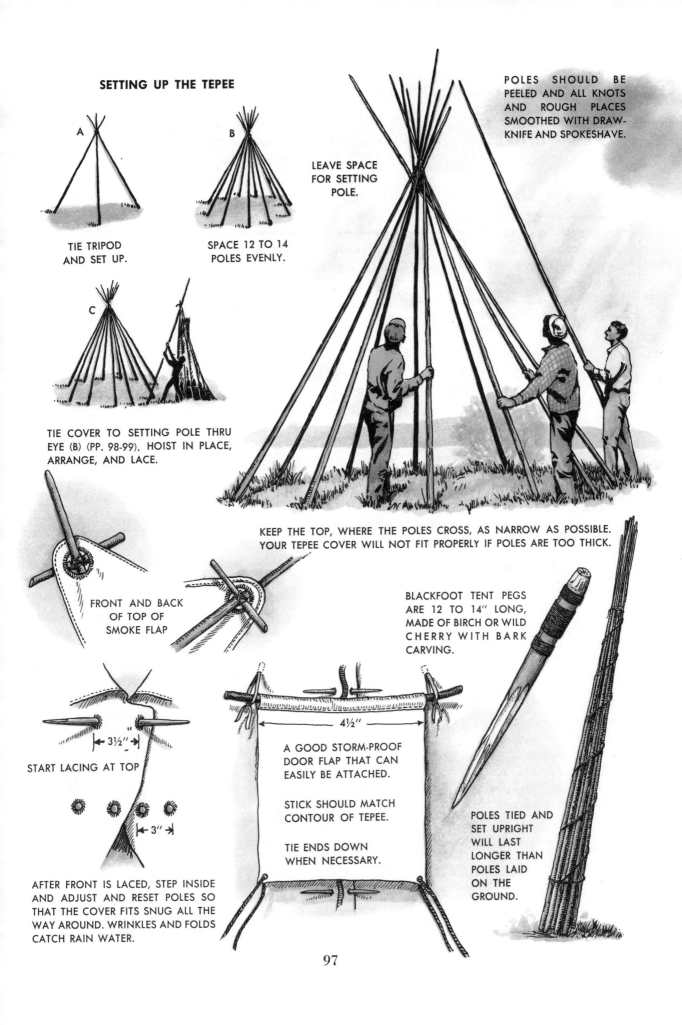

SETTING UP THE TEPEE

A

TIE TRIPOD
AND SET UP.

B

SPACE 12 TO 14
POLES EVENLY.

LEAVE SPACE
FOR SETTING
POLE.

POLES SHOULD BE
PEELED AND ALL KNOTS
AND ROUGH PLACES
SMOOTHED WITH DRAW-
KNIFE AND SPOKESHAVE.

C

TIE COVER TO SETTING POLE THRU
EYE (B) (PP. 98-99). HOIST IN PLACE,
ARRANGE, AND LACE.

KEEP THE TOP, WHERE THE POLES CROSS, AS NARROW AS POSSIBLE.
YOUR TEPEE COVER WILL NOT FIT PROPERLY IF POLES ARE TOO THICK.

FRONT AND BACK
OF TOP OF
SMOKE FLAP

BLACKFOOT TENT PEGS
ARE 12 TO 14" LONG,
MADE OF BIRCH OR WILD
CHERRY WITH BARK
CARVING.

←3½"→

START LACING AT TOP

←3"→

AFTER FRONT IS LACED, STEP INSIDE
AND ADJUST AND RESET POLES SO
THAT THE COVER FITS SNUG ALL THE
WAY AROUND. WRINKLES AND FOLDS
CATCH RAIN WATER.

←——— 4½" ———→

A GOOD STORM-PROOF
DOOR FLAP THAT CAN
EASILY BE ATTACHED.

STICK SHOULD MATCH
CONTOUR OF TEPEE.

TIE ENDS DOWN
WHEN NECESSARY.

POLES TIED AND
SET UPRIGHT
WILL LAST
LONGER THAN
POLES LAID
ON THE
GROUND.

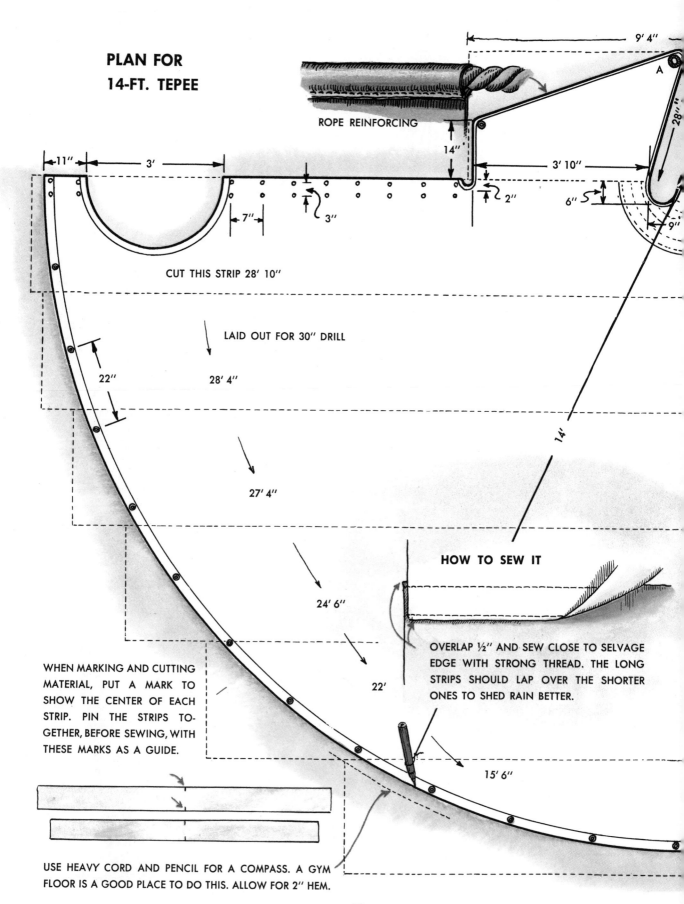

**PLAN FOR
14-FT. TEPEE**

ROPE REINFORCING

9' 4"

A

28"

14"

11"   3'   3' 10"   2"   6'   9"

7"   3"

CUT THIS STRIP 28' 10"

LAID OUT FOR 30" DRILL

22"   28' 4"

14'

27' 4"

HOW TO SEW IT

24' 6"

OVERLAP ½" AND SEW CLOSE TO SELVAGE
EDGE WITH STRONG THREAD. THE LONG
STRIPS SHOULD LAP OVER THE SHORTER
ONES TO SHED RAIN BETTER.

22'

WHEN MARKING AND CUTTING
MATERIAL, PUT A MARK TO
SHOW THE CENTER OF EACH
STRIP. PIN THE STRIPS TO-
GETHER, BEFORE SEWING, WITH
THESE MARKS AS A GUIDE.

15' 6"

USE HEAVY CORD AND PENCIL FOR A COMPASS. A GYM
FLOOR IS A GOOD PLACE TO DO THIS. ALLOW FOR 2" HEM.

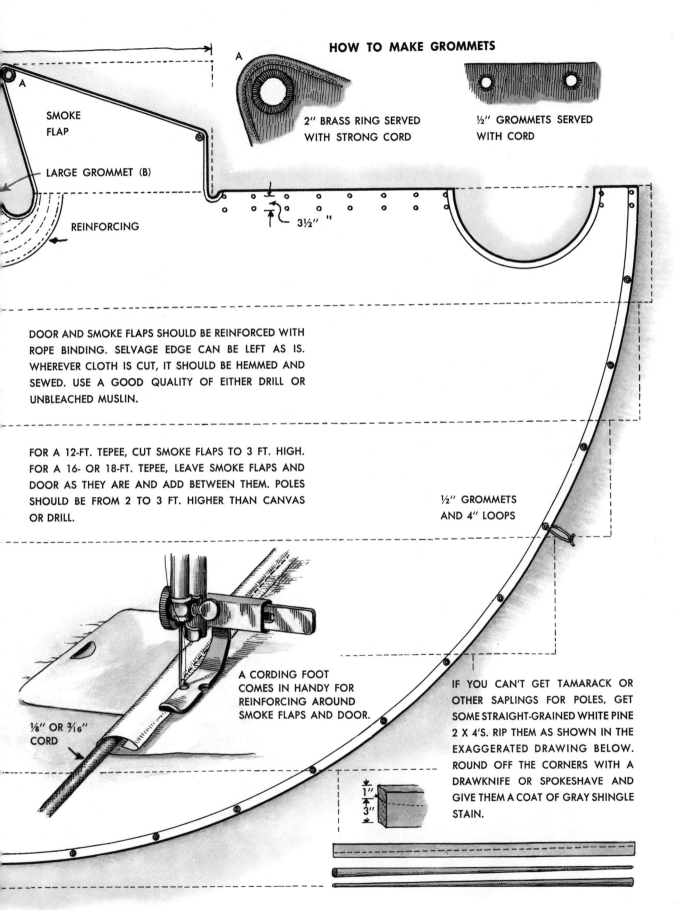

HOW TO MAKE GROMMETS

SMOKE
FLAP

2" BRASS RING SERVED
WITH STRONG CORD

½" GROMMETS SERVED
WITH CORD

LARGE GROMMET (B)

REINFORCING

3½ "

DOOR AND SMOKE FLAPS SHOULD BE REINFORCED WITH
ROPE BINDING. SELVAGE EDGE CAN BE LEFT AS IS.
WHEREVER CLOTH IS CUT, IT SHOULD BE HEMMED AND
SEWED. USE A GOOD QUALITY OF EITHER DRILL OR
UNBLEACHED MUSLIN.

FOR A 12-FT. TEPEE, CUT SMOKE FLAPS TO 3 FT. HIGH.
FOR A 16- OR 18-FT. TEPEE, LEAVE SMOKE FLAPS AND
DOOR AS THEY ARE AND ADD BETWEEN THEM. POLES
SHOULD BE FROM 2 TO 3 FT. HIGHER THAN CANVAS
OR DRILL.

½" GROMMETS
AND 4" LOOPS

A CORDING FOOT
COMES IN HANDY FOR
REINFORCING AROUND
SMOKE FLAPS AND DOOR.

⅛" OR ³⁄₁₆"
CORD

IF YOU CAN'T GET TAMARACK OR
OTHER SAPLINGS FOR POLES, GET
SOME STRAIGHT-GRAINED WHITE PINE
2 X 4'S. RIP THEM AS SHOWN IN THE
EXAGGERATED DRAWING BELOW.
ROUND OFF THE CORNERS WITH A
DRAWKNIFE OR SPOKESHAVE AND
GIVE THEM A COAT OF GRAY SHINGLE
STAIN.

1"
3"

TEPEE DESIGNS

Before you paint designs on your tepee, you will have to spread it on the floor and spray it with a good waterproofing material. After this dries, you can decorate the tepee with designs which will identify it as yours. Refer to the designs on pp. 66-69 for ideas. The designs used by the Indians were partly geometric and were usually based on dreams of the owner. Often the owner's totem was painted on the door flap.

Red, yellow, black, green, and white are all good tepee colors. Cobalt blue or ultra marine are attractive, but remember that all blues fade quickly. Paint the bottom a dark color so that it will not show the dirt. Use thinned house paint.

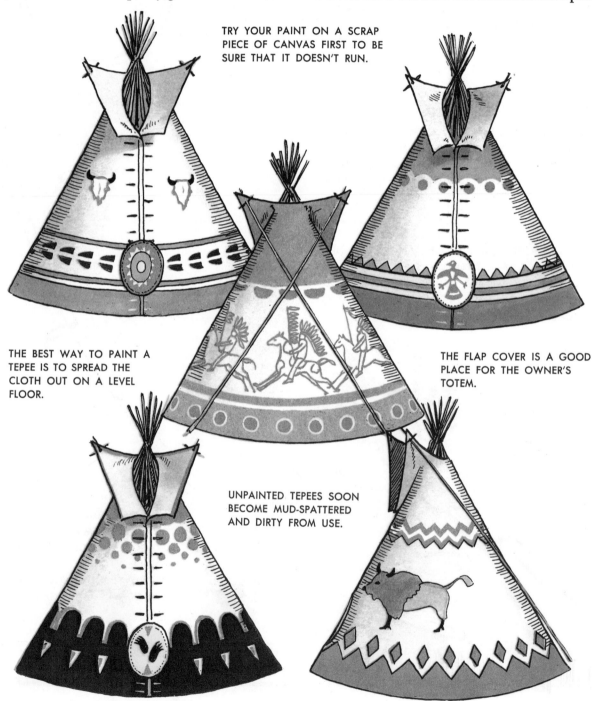

TRY YOUR PAINT ON A SCRAP PIECE OF CANVAS FIRST TO BE SURE THAT IT DOESN'T RUN.

THE BEST WAY TO PAINT A TEPEE IS TO SPREAD THE CLOTH OUT ON A LEVEL FLOOR.

THE FLAP COVER IS A GOOD PLACE FOR THE OWNER'S TOTEM.

UNPAINTED TEPEES SOON BECOME MUD-SPATTERED AND DIRTY FROM USE.

TEPEE DEW~CLOTH

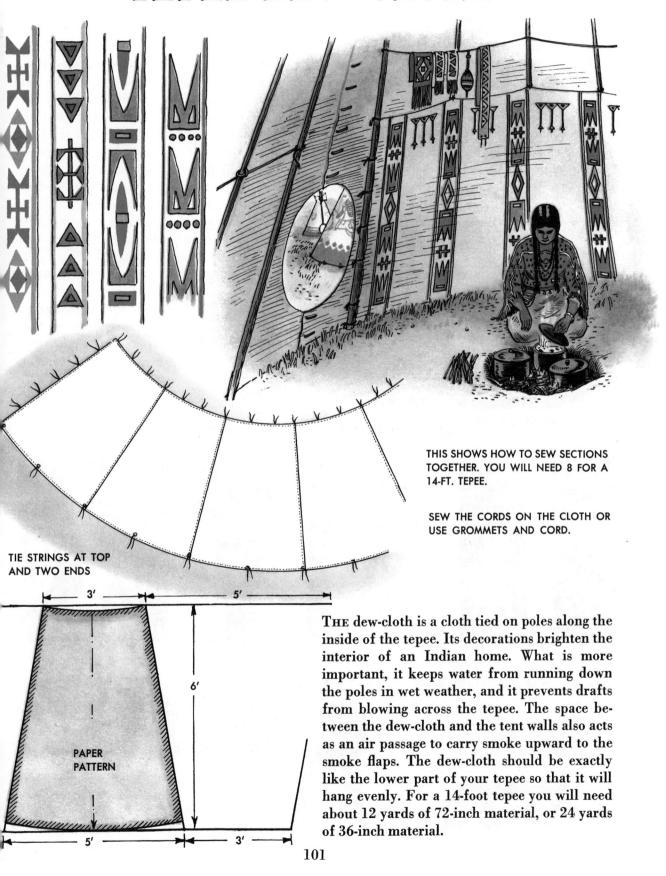

THIS SHOWS HOW TO SEW SECTIONS TOGETHER. YOU WILL NEED 8 FOR A 14-FT. TEPEE.

SEW THE CORDS ON THE CLOTH OR USE GROMMETS AND CORD.

TIE STRINGS AT TOP AND TWO ENDS

PAPER PATTERN

THE dew-cloth is a cloth tied on poles along the inside of the tepee. Its decorations brighten the interior of an Indian home. What is more important, it keeps water from running down the poles in wet weather, and it prevents drafts from blowing across the tepee. The space between the dew-cloth and the tent walls also acts as an air passage to carry smoke upward to the smoke flaps. The dew-cloth should be exactly like the lower part of your tepee so that it will hang evenly. For a 14-foot tepee you will need about 12 yards of 72-inch material, or 24 yards of 36-inch material.

101

TOTEM POLES

THE Indian tribes living along the river valleys and on the offshore islands from northern Washington to Alaska are called the Northwest Coast tribes. They are noted for their wood-carving, particularly for their totem poles. These carved cedar poles were originally corner posts for the Indian houses. Later the custom of erecting one large pole in front of the house was adopted. There are several different types of totem poles. Some were erected to the memory of the dead. Others portrayed the owner's family tree or illustrated some mythological adventure.

The poles varied in height from about 40 to 70 feet. The larger ones were as much as 3 feet in diameter. The carver was an important person in his tribe. For his work he might be paid from one hundred to two hundred and fifty blankets, each worth about three dollars. The early poles were painted black, white, and red. Other colors were used when the traders brought in factory-made paints.

Carving a pole is a very good project for a group of boys. By following the instructions on these two pages you can make a totem pole that will have all the earmarks of one made by the Indians. To start, get an old telephone pole that you can clean up by removing about ½ inch of the outside wood. A green bass or pine log will carve very nicely. Authentic Northwest designs, such as those on this page, should be used. Poles with from one to four design units seem to work out best. To make a totem pole takes time and patience, but the results are well worth the effort.

KEEP YOUR TOOLS SHARP AT ALL TIMES.

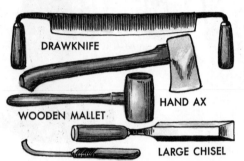

DRAWKNIFE

HAND AX

WOODEN MALLET

LARGE CHISEL

CROOKED KNIFE

DESIGNS FROM OLD TOTEM POLES

FRONT   SIDE

1. FIRST CHOP AWAY ABOUT ONE THIRD OF THE BACK OF THE POLE AND SMOOTH WITH A DRAWKNIFE.

2. PLACE POLE ON SAW HORSES TO BRING IT ABOUT HIP HIGH. CLEAN UP WITH DRAWKNIFE.

3. THEN LAY OUT THE DESIGNS YOU WISH TO USE WITH WAX CRAYON OR HEAVY SOFT PENCIL. ONLY THE MAIN PARTS ARE MARKED. DON'T WORRY ABOUT A FEW CRACKS.

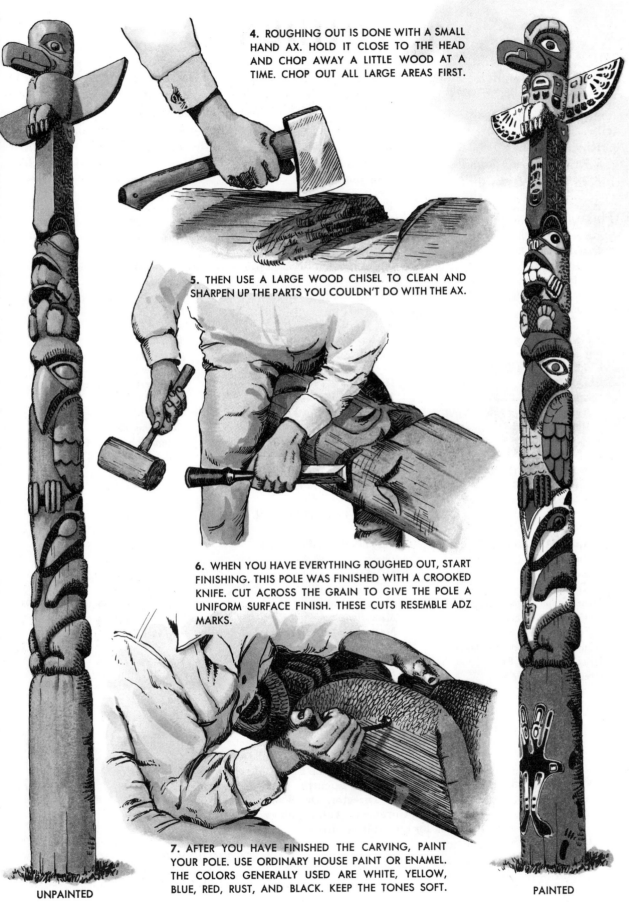

4. ROUGHING OUT IS DONE WITH A SMALL HAND AX. HOLD IT CLOSE TO THE HEAD AND CHOP AWAY A LITTLE WOOD AT A TIME. CHOP OUT ALL LARGE AREAS FIRST.

5. THEN USE A LARGE WOOD CHISEL TO CLEAN AND SHARPEN UP THE PARTS YOU COULDN'T DO WITH THE AX.

6. WHEN YOU HAVE EVERYTHING ROUGHED OUT, START FINISHING. THIS POLE WAS FINISHED WITH A CROOKED KNIFE. CUT ACROSS THE GRAIN TO GIVE THE POLE A UNIFORM SURFACE FINISH. THESE CUTS RESEMBLE ADZ MARKS.

7. AFTER YOU HAVE FINISHED THE CARVING, PAINT YOUR POLE. USE ORDINARY HOUSE PAINT OR ENAMEL. THE COLORS GENERALLY USED ARE WHITE, YELLOW, BLUE, RED, RUST, AND BLACK. KEEP THE TONES SOFT.

UNPAINTED

PAINTED

103

INDEX

AUTHOR'S ACKNOWLEDGMENT

I WISH to thank the Milwaukee Public Museum for many years of assistance in furnishing scientific data on the American Indian, and especially its Director, Dr. W. C. McKern, and Mr. R. E. Ritzenthaler, Curator of Anthropology, for their aid in checking this book for scientific accuracy.

LONE
EAGLE

WANBLEE
ISNALA

ABCD